# Folk Opposition

# Folk Opposition

Alex Niven

Winchester, UK
Washington, USA

First published by Zero Books, 2012
Zero Books is an imprint of John Hunt Publishing Ltd., Laurel House, Station Approach,
Alresford, Hants, SO24 9JH, UK
office1@o-books.net
www.o-books.com

For distributor details and how to order please visit the 'Ordering' section on our website.

Text copyright: Alex Niven 2010

ISBN: 978 1 78099 032 3

A CIP catalogue record for this book is available from the British Library.

Design: Stuart Davies

Printed in the UK by CPI Antony Rowe
Printed in the USA by Offset Paperback Mfrs, Inc

We operate a distinctive and ethical publishing philosophy in all
areas of our business, from our global network of authors to
production and worldwide distribution.

# CONTENTS

*I praise your good intentions sir,*
*I love your kind and gentle heart*
*But now it's 1842,*
*And you and I we're miles apart.*

*A hundred years and more will pass*
*Before we're standing side by side*
*But please accept my grateful thanks:*
*God bless you sir, at least you tried.*

– The Unthanks, The Testimony of Patience Kershaw
(written by Frank Higgins, 1969).

# Foreword

This short book examines the old, basic idea of a fundamental opposition between rulers and ruled, between a powerful elite and a disempowered populace. This is a book that explores a renewed divide between ordinary folk and an exploitative sovereignty.

For many people there will be something unavoidably sentimental and reductive about the idea that such a thing as a folk even exists in the twenty-first century. Yet the whole point of the following argument is to defend the idea of broadness, of commonality, even – perhaps above all – of sentiment. The denial of folk sentiment, the denial of a common history and heritage, is one way in which popular opposition and resistance to rising inequality and a widespread revival of hierarchy has been slowly erased over the last thirty years. While neoliberalism has increasingly resorted to profoundly old-fashioned, irrational myths in its defence of individual interest and private wealth, it has paradoxically dismissed all group-based identities as outdated and oppressive. Ancient monarchies enjoy glamorous revivals; meanwhile, twentieth century phrases like "social democracy," "unionisation", and "solidarity" can scarcely be uttered without inviting accusations of nostalgia. Establishment sentiment is good for tourism and national unity; folk sentiment is the preserve of neo-fascists and hoary socialist ideologues.

So it is less a question of moving with the times than a case of which version of history is being invoked. Despite the contemporary obsession with modernisation, in many ways, as we shall see, Britain has reverted to a pre-twentieth century, pre-labour movement climate in which a liberal-conservative elite rules over a deeply divided, individualistic culture, one in which the means of representation are everywhere withheld from the general population in a way that seems strikingly old-fashioned. Against this backdrop, it seems sensible to suggest that nothing can even begin to be remedied unless a basic commitment to an oppositional collective ideal is somehow revived. This book offers the word "folk" as one provisional way of defining that ideal.

The first section presents a broad overview of a culture in which deepening social division has been the inevitable consequence of a privatised economy. In the second section, the co-option of folk and roots motifs by the New Tory ascendancy is examined. The second half of the book takes a slight detour to examine the role of place and regional identity in determining an oppositional outlook. The first of these chapters treats the north-east of England as an example of a place where folk sentiment and popular opposition to the English establishment remain meaningful quotidian notions. The final section looks at the football culture of the north-east and the emergence of the supporters' trust movement, and suggests that a bottom-up revival of collective action might be a natural response to the increasingly visible corruptions of a reckless capitalist power elite.

Even without taking into account the vast inequalities that exist on a global scale, it is clear that we are living in an age of profound anti-egalitarianism and loneliness. In our own country, there is an underworld of suffering lurking beneath a surface-world of consumerist fantasy and lifestyle myths. The essential assertion of the following essay is that the best way to counteract this climate of negativity and radical privacy is through a socialism that is founded in the extraordinary potential of the ordinary, the populist, the community level, the everyday, a socialism that derives its identity from a simple belief that we are better off in teams than we are as isolated individuals.

In an important sense this can be no more than a belief. One compelling reason for investing faith in collective over individual interests is that we simply won't be able to carry on for very long if we continue to separate ourselves off into atom-sized pockets where nothing matters but our own private interests. Yet other than this very general instinct for self-preservation, it is ultimately belief and not an overweening rationality that will lead us to see solidarity with others as the most essential aspect of our being. We can lay a foundation for this in reason, but even our most intelligent reasonings will fall away into relativist meaninglessness if we don't also learn how to talk with simple, sincere clarity about the fundamentals that underwrite our most elaborate political theories.

This book is dedicated to the memory of my dad, who on NUFC match days would buy me a copy of *The Mag*, or *Socialist Worker*, or a CD, or a novel. And also to the memory of my mum, who taught me that fantastic hope is the greatest of all virtues.

I

# Two Britains

*And even those who still have the power to cry out, the cry hardly ever expresses itself, either inwardly or outwardly, in coherent language. Usually the words through which it seeks expression are quite irrelevant.*

*That is all the more inevitable because those who most often have occasion to feel that evil is being done to them are those who are least trained in the art of speech. Nothing, for example, is more frightful than to see some poor wretch in the police court stammering before a magistrate who keeps up an elegant flow of witticisms.*

- Simone Weil, "Human Personality".

## Raoul and David

In July 2010, the recently released prisoner and sometime nightclub doorman Raoul Moat committed suicide by shooting himself in the head, after a long police manhunt in and around the village of Rothbury in Northumberland. Night vision footage of Moat's last moments was broadcast around the globe, a suitably uncanny climax to a narrative that had at times seemed to be taking place on another planet.

For all its remoteness, Rothbury can scarcely be described as a backwater. In the late-nineteenth century the Victorian armaments magnate Lord Armstrong recruited the architect Norman Shaw to build the extravagant, proto-consumerist paradise that is Cragside - the first electrically lit house in the world - on the outskirts of the village. Nevertheless, Moat's dramatic final fling and the accompanying media farrago temporarily made Northumberland look like a mythical hinterland, a modern-day Wild West or a British outback, with a pathological Geordie skinhead standing in for Billy the Kid or Ned Kelly. As if to underline this, certain members of the London media seemed to view Rothbury as a sort of virgin colonial terrain, a theme park for indulging in gung ho, Boys Own-style behaviour. Halfway through the manhunt, Channel 4 correspondent Alex Thomson posted a breathlessly excited message to his Twitter page: "sorry lots of Bberry tweets in dark running thru peoples gardens evading cops – some spelling may have gone astray."Another Tweet, from Sky News's James Matthews, was just as fantastically unhinged: "Was listening to negotiations till armed cop found us. Crept up silently, first I knew was when I felt his breath on my cheek."

Moat was a dangerous criminal on a paranoid mission to "punish" his ex-girlfriend for alleged infidelity, and to visit vengeance on a mystified projection of "powers that be." Yet bizarrely, perhaps because his opponents in the police and media seemed so reprehensible, Moat quickly acquired the status of a folk hero in some isolated quarters, particularly in the north-east. During and after the manhunt, Facebook groups celebrating "Moat the legend" began to appear. (Other epithets on discussion boards included "warrior," "martyr," and, most surreally of all, "the British Mandela.") The site of Moat's last stand was laden with flowers and messages of sympathy. Meanwhile, *The Sun* reported that a section of the crowd at a pre-season football friendly between Newcastle United and Carlisle had chanted "Raoul Moat, he's our friend, he shoots coppers."[1] The most tragicomic instance of pro-Moat sentiment occurred during the manhunt itself, when ex-England footballer Paul Gascoigne turned up in Rothbury with a can of lager and a roast chicken, determined to have a chat and go for a fish with his old drinking pal "Moaty." He was, according to Gazza, a nice lad once you got to know him.

The recently elected Prime Minister and sometime hereditary

millionaire David Cameron, however, saw things slightly differently. Days after Moat's death, Cameron stood up during Prime Minister's Questions to offer a categorical, "full stop, end of story" dismissal of support for the "callous murderer." "I cannot understand any wave, however small, of public sympathy for this man," said Cameron, to vigorous cheers of assent from all around the House.

In debunking some of the absurdities of the Moat affair, Cameron showed a modicum of good sense. Even the liberal journalist John Tatlock, in a piece for *The Quietus* music website, judged Cameron's comments to be "pithily accurate," and attached a Spotify playlist with the theme "how folk heroism warps reality," featuring tunes by Nick Cave and N.W.A.[2] Whether it was Old Tory rectitude or soundbite opportunism which prompted Cameron to anathematise Moat, he seemed to have caught the mood of a sizeable constituency of Britons. Cameron delighted in the role of the rational, righteous man of the hour, the polar opposite of his demonic counterpart (and rival for column inches) the unequivocally evil thug Raoul Moat. As the cultural critic Mark Fisher pointed out with smart eloquence on his k-punk blog, this was Britain's Anti-Diana Moment. Cameron had struck a timely nerve, just as Tony Blair had done back in 1997 with his theatrically emotive TV appearance in the wake of Diana's death.

But which public was Cameron speaking for when he so emphatically damned Moat to an afterlife devoid of sympathy? If Blair's address to the nation in '97 had embodied all the pseudo-populism and Augustan glamour of the late-nineties New Labour zeitgeist, then what did Cameron's no-nonsense attack on Moat and his sympathisers say about a Britain heading into the 2010s under the New Tories? In his demagogic early phase, Blair had projected an air of almost maniacal empathy, riffing incessantly on his genial "People's Prince" persona. So Cameron's candid admission that he *could not understand* the public reaction to the Moat affair was interesting. While Blair had presented a masterly brand-image of centrist unity, a pragmatic compromise after the ideological polarities of the eighties, Cameron, though no less calculated and Machiavellian than Blair, was notably less concerned with being all things to all people. In fact, he seemed remarkably comfortable with the fact of there being an insurmountable opposition between himself and a marginal fringe of his own electorate.

Underneath the tabloid stereotypes of the Moat affair, what sort of opposition was this? Again, it must be repeated that Moat was a reprehensible, psychopathic killer. But why did so many ordinary people seem to take his side, however briefly and flippantly, and why did Cameron see fit to dismiss these people with such unforgiving vehemence?

## The Big Society and The Great Divide

In some respects, Cameron's unambiguous response to the Moat affair was a surprise. After all, the central motif of the Conservative's 2010 election campaign had been the so-called Big Society, a brazenly populist initiative designed to win over just enough ordinary folk to swing a tight race. The precise nature of the Big Society – a near-scandalous homage to FDR's hardcore statist Great Society – was, and remains, a mystery[3]. Nevertheless, it is often highlighted as a neo-Blairite maneuver on Cameron's part, a stab at "progressivism" passed-over by many traditional Tories as a hollow gimmick (though it is perhaps the ring of egalitarianism that is their real bone of contention). The Big Society's prominent position in the foreground of Conservative PR during the election was a firm indication that Cameron saw himself as the natural heir to Blair, a realpolitik pragmatist with the added sugarcoating of a penchant for earthy, man-of-the-people initiatives. Somehow, Cameron managed to cast himself as a compassionate-conservative antidote to Westminster elitism. The MP's expenses scandal, quite obviously an indictment of all three parties, redounded mainly on Gordon Brown's head. Meanwhile, Cameron made significant approaches to the yeoman folk of England with his bathetic common sense and canny communicability. If anyone captured the public imagination during the 2010 election, it was Cameron, albeit in the manner of a mildy risible "folk-hero" who made embarrassingly ersatz speeches to "communities" of assembled London journalists.

Cameron's post-election coalition pact with the superlatively nice-but-vapid Lib Dem leader Nick Clegg – his major rival for public esteem - seemed like final confirmation of his progressive-populist stance. But soon the mask began to slip. This was not, like the late-nineties, a time when the myth of things getting better for an increasingly capacious middle-mass of the populace had been the hallmark of New Labour un-ideology. The dire economic climate called for decisive action based on a foundation of clearly defined principles, even if those principles were obscured by the deployment of classic neoliberal cloaking devices such as "pragmatism," "progressivism," and "getting things done, for the sake of the country."

In short, despite the illusion of a coalition built on utilitarian compromise, the situation called for an ideological taking of sides, and it quickly became apparent what those sides would look like. Cameron's total lack of understanding for the sympathy shown by north-easterners towards Raoul Moat showed up the fact that, when it came down to it, he really wasn't too bothered about alienating people outside the traditional Tory base, particularly disenfranchised working class northerners misguidedly championing anyone at all offering a semblance of anti-Establishment assertiveness, even in the form of a hapless sociopath.

If the Moat affair was an extreme example of the limits of Cameronian sympathy, there were other signs of a renewed oppositional orientation in Tory policy. Even before the election,

Cameron had been explicit in declaring the north-east and Northern Ireland to be two places where the state had "got too big", places where there needed to be a "bigger private sector." In the absence of any concrete programme for new private investment in these regions, this translated to an out and out admission that the expected Thatcher-style jobs cull would have a specific geographic and socio-economic focus. A few months previously, the Conservative Party think-tank Policy Exchange had declared that upwardly mobile residents of places like Sunderland, Bradford, and Liverpool should give up on their hometowns as lost causes and migrate to the prosperous south-east. Meanwhile, there was an almost deafening absence in Tory rhetoric of any attacks whatsoever on more affluent locales, such as, say, the City of London. This was hardly the One Nationism one might expect from a party desperate to project itself as a progressive, moderate successor to New Labour. Clearly, divide and rule politics were still very much at the heart of the New Tory identity.

How were people in the north-east expected to react to such patrician disdain for their livelihoods? Is it any wonder that a small minority would side with Raoul Moat over a man intent on decimating their communities while defending the interests of a south-eastern elite emerging unscathed from a financial crisis largely of its own making?

## The New Plutocracy
Of course, it is not only Cameron and the New Tories that have become progressively distanced from the constituency that, on its extreme fringes, dared to express sympathy for Raoul Moat. Both the outgoing New Labour government and the incoming Conservative-Lib Dem coalition were effusive in their proclamations of loyalty to the political centre, and hence to an unmistakably small-c conservative preservation of a neoliberal status quo which inevitably rewards some at the expense of others.

What is new about Cameron is that he exposes the spuriousness of the notion that a "centrist" political consensus equates to an equable toleration of diverse interest groups, a kind of magic-formula egalitarian unity from which no one is excluded. Cameron has in a sense provided a public service, exposing the latent polarities of latter-day British society that were for a long time buried underneath an obfuscating hailstorm of New Labour PR paradoxes (we're the party of equality but we're supremely relaxed about people getting filthy rich; we believe passionately in the public sector but don't mind hammering teachers and lecturers with low pay, league tables, and the nightmare of neo-Stalinist bureaucracy; Gordon Brown will be a great friend of the developing world while staunchly advocating the interests of global capital; and so on and so forth).

Indeed, Cameron arrived on the scene against the backdrop of a long-running political consensus that feigns centrist neutrality while maintaining a cast-iron bias in favour of a specific societal group: a new plutocracy every bit as self-regarding and imperious as plutocracies of the past. In many ways, modern politics has come to resemble the pre-Labour movement Whig/Tory divide of the 18th and 19th centuries, with two parties representing different divisions of a sizeable wealthy class. On one hand is the traditional New Right base of businessmen, accountants, bankers, estate agents, most of whom vote Conservative, sometimes New Labour or Lib Dem. But this is now joined by a "new new money" demographic (those working in the entertainment and leisure industries, the media, marketing, advertising, the so-called "creative industries", managerial-class public sector workers) most of whom vote Lib Dem or New Labour, sometimes Conservative. Together with the traditional old money demographic, the real aristocracy and the monolithic squirearchy of farmers and small landowners who will always vote Conservative no matter what, these three groups combine to form a formidable power monopoly.

Economic, political, and cultural bases are all covered with alarming totality.

While the elusive nature of the new plutocracy is partially the result of a postmodern climate in which identities blur and it is difficult to work out who is being exploited by whom, the basic fact of its existence is certainly nothing new. As George Orwell commented in 1941:

> After 1832 the old land-owning aristocracy steadily lost power, but instead of disappearing or becoming a fossil they simply intermarried with the merchants, manufacturers and financiers who had replaced them, and soon turned them into accurate copies of themselves. The wealthy shipowner or cotton-miller set up for himself an alibi as a country gentleman, while his sons learned the right mannerisms at public schools which had been designed for just that purpose. England was ruled by an aristocracy constantly recruited from parvenus[4].

Orwell's remarks remind us that contemporary developments merely extend a time-honoured British tradition: the absorption by the ruling elite of enterprising *arriviste* classes. This social dynamic has predominated in England and the UK since at least the Glorious Revolution of 1688, probably as far back as the late-Middle Ages, and it has never been substantially altered. Old and new money are recurrently elided, successively bolstered over the centuries by comparative internal stability and more-or-less uninterrupted economic and political dominance on a global scale. Britain has never really relinquished its position as one of the world's most imperiously powerful societies, for all the talk of a "decline" in the late-twentieth century. And, whether it is Empire, international free trade, or latter-day globalised consumer capitalism that is setting the dominant tone, the Imperium of the day must cast the net wide when recruiting its taskmasters. The incorporation of the lower middle class and a top echelon of the working class into New Right-base commercial and business professions, and more recently, the rise of New Labour-base "creative" and leisure sectors and the business-aping public sector managerial class, is merely the latest installment in a centuries-old narrative.

In such a way, Britain's anti-egalitarian internal social makeup is continually renewed by the illusion that things can only get better for everyone, while a select group of ambitious *nouveau* social climbers quietly slides into the existing power network on the sly. Everyone recognises the old Establishment of stock-brokers, executives, and privately educated politicians. But a remarkable triumph of the new plutocracy has been to siphon off that portion of the upper-working and lower-middle class – the intellectually and artistically fertile "liminal class," to borrow the music journalist Simon Reynolds's useful phrase - so that it too becomes an organ of elite self-propagation. Indie (formerly "independent") musicians now live in Notting Hill mansions with Hollywood celebrity wives. University arts courses are populated with bright, fashion-obsessed young men and women securing low 2:1 degrees before going to work for large accountancy firms or nebulous London marketing agencies. A huge demand for jobs in the media and entertainment industry fosters a culture of nepotism in which it is usually the most affluent and best-connected private and grammar school-educated south-easterners that manage to secure gainful employment.

These are Blair's children, the constituents of a new elite. A notable problem is that their existence and dominance is perhaps only really visible to those on the outside of the circle, like the north-easterners who left flowers at the scene of Raoul Moat's death after macho public schoolboy journalists had literally trampled all over their back gardens.

## The Redundant Population

*And when we see the lower classes of the English people uniformly singled out as marks for the malice or servility of a certain description of writers – when we see them studiously separated, like a degraded* caste, *from the rest of the community, with scarcely the attributes and faculties of the species allowed them ... when we see the* redundant population *(as it is fashionably called) selected as the butt for every paltry effusion of spite ... when we are accustomed to hear the poor, the uninformed, the friendless, put, by tacit consent, out of the pale of society ... when they are familiarly spoken of as a sort of vermin only fit to be hunted down, and exterminated at the discretion of their betters: – we know pretty well what to think, both of the disinterestedness of the motives which give currency to this jargon, and of the wisdom of the policy which should either sanction, or suffer itself to be influenced by its suggestions.*

- William Hazlitt, "Capital Punishments" (1821).

All three parties aim to win over a large enough portion of the new plutocracy to be able to govern, leaving a great swathe of the British electorate with little or no real enfranchisement in mainstream politics: a vast "other constituency".

Typically, members of the other constituency work in the public sector (teachers, nurses, council workers, old-school university lecturers) or they are members of the "old working class" (traditional manual jobs, and, increasingly, call centre workers, cleaners, service industry menial jobs), or they are unemployed. Most of this group vote Labour, sometimes Lib Dem, occasionally Conservative, but more often don't vote at all, either because they are disillusioned with politicians, because they feel betrayed by the rightward drift of the Labour Party, or because they simply couldn't care less. All three parties make token concessionary approaches to this constituency – Cameron's "Big Society", New Labour's moderate achievements in establishing a minimum wage, all three "talking tough" on immigration, etc – but they mostly don't bother much with these people, because they only have to be won over in very small numbers to clinch an election victory, and because they usually have fairly entrenched political loyalties anyway (invariably "Old Labour," which means a default vote for Labour or no vote at all).

It should go without saying that life has been getting pretty grim for the members of this other constituency for some time now. In former manufacturing towns, the unemployed coexist with the barely employed and the imminently out-of-work (a situation that is already being hugely exacerbated by Cameron's direct attacks on "public sector areas"). Teachers, social workers, and health care professionals carry the can of market-style progress initiatives and shrill exhortations to "be better" and "do more with less," while they watch their private-sector middle-class coevals flourish on astronomical salaries. Low-income families in fragmented communities offload resentment onto their immediate neighbours who have managed to buy a handful of expensive new toys with a meagre child benefit allowance. Meanwhile, the long-term unemployed endure the agony, addiction, and mental health problems that are the eternal curses of the unemployed, and immigrants swell the ranks of a revitalised sex industry or die anonymously doing nineteenth-century-style menial jobs on northern beaches.

Part of the problem is that, like the new plutocracy, the other constituency remains an inchoate amalgam of disparate groups, lacking either political representation or the sort of self-conscious identity that was provided by unions and cooperative organizations in days gone by. It is difficult to see any sort of united front is to be achieved in a society totally lacking anything approaching a common culture. On the surface of it, what shared ground is there between, say, a Polish teenager working in a sandwich shop and a fifty-something sixth-form college lecturer, or between a nurse in Dundee and an unemployed man in Portsmouth? The old variety of national class-consciousness described by historians like E.P. Thompson, Eric Hobsbawm, and Richard Hoggart in the mid-twentieth century, embodied in signifiers such as the flat cap, the fish and chip shop, and the Saturday football match, represents a form of collective symbolism that can only be dreamed of in a modern Britain thoroughly atomised by the acquisitive individualism of neoliberal economics[5]. With the right-wing media maintaining a perpetual babble of wholly unfounded anti-union rhetoric, the prospect of the other constituency achieving even a basic level of collective unity appears quite bleak[6].

Without any really effective grassroots institutions to give coherence to an extremely varied demographic, the descent into anarchic confusion and internalised, self-directed violence becomes predictable. A lack of solidarity very quickly turns into hostility to the nearest visible target, and the narcissism of small difference leads people to vent rage on the people closest to home. At the extremist end of the spectrum, Raoul Moat mutilates his girlfriend and murders her lover, while the middle-aged taxi driver Derrick Bird slaughters his twin brother and proceeds to kill eleven other arbitrary community members in a remote corner of West Cumbria.

## Hard Times in the Media

Again, it must be re-asserted that *representation* of all forms, in mainstream politics, in culture, and especially in the media, is one of the central factors in a dynamic that is spectacularly rigged in favour of the plutocratic middle-mass. On the other hand, members of the other constituency are reduced to Victorian caricatures if they are depicted at all. The standout noughties state-of-the-nation comedy series was *Little Britain*. Its portraits of the redundant population combined superficial Dickensian social observation with an almost pathological lack of real sympathy for the archetypes being lampooned. Vicky Pollard, the epochal "chav," was stupid, inarticulate, and recalcitrant, her Bristol accent a reminder that Matt Lucas and David Walliams had both studied at the ultra-elite University of Bristol, a bastion of Home Counties hegemony and social separatism. Pollard's portrayal was exactly the view of the privileged *flaneur* student who has accidentally wandered out of Georgian Clifton and found himself lost on the local housing estate.

But where Dickens deployed a similar cartoon-vignette device at the same time as offering a liberal-radical critique of the social conditions that had created his urban grotesques, Walliams and Lucas had no such scruples. In fact, they were apolitical metrosexuals who carved out a niche as darlings of the London celebrity party scene. These were scarcely figures in a position to make the sort of wide-ranging observations necessary for social-realistic portraiture, even of a broadly satirical kind. As with working class teenagers (see also Daffyd Thomas, the "only gay in the village"), *Little Britain's* portraits of care workers and the disabled (Lou and Andy) and elderly northerners (Roy and Margeret) were utterly flat and ungenerous[7]. That the show also poked fun at ridiculous upper class idiots could not really compensate for the fact that the one group not being attacked was the metropolitan elite from which its creators had emerged. Within this demographic, and in British cultural life as a whole, sympathy for the Other was on the slide.

The mid-to-late twentieth century seemed to promise a new atmosphere of egalitarianism. A flourishing popular culture provided a humane expression of a society in which the longtime voiceless were finally finding a voice, through new media like pop music, social realism, and television. But as social mobility has fallen by the wayside over the last three decades, popular culture has increasingly resorted to mystified, nineteenth century-style stereotyping in its depiction of marginal social groups. Even the nineties allowed for Oasis, Pulp, and Irvine

Welsh. But even such amgbiguous representatives of working class identity as these figures do not have parallels in the new century, one in which Simon Cowell, Alan Sugar, and Andrew Lloyd-Webber are openly lauded as popular figures, without even having to make a show of disguising their inordinate wealth and class accoutrements[8]. Meanwhile, closer to the liberal centre, the sybaritic cosmopolitanism of the Williamses and Lucases is occluded: they are still notionally "alternative comics," apparently anti-conservative on the surface, while remaining paid-up members of a wealthy and influential power elite in actuality. Their surrealist-nihilist variety of "radicalism" is about as subversive as it gets, and it is unremittingly – even self-consciously – upper-middle class.

If *Little Britain* gave expression to a warped, top-down view of the British populace, an atmosphere of selfishness and nastiness persisted in countless other popular culture artifacts of the '00s. Negative solidarity and self-directed bitterness were the hallmarks of '00s pop cultural life, which marked a sea change from the happy consciousness of the early-Blairite era. Destiny's Child set the tone for the ensuing decade when they released "Independent Woman" in 2000, the chorus of which set new standards of ultra-Thatcherite, self-worshipping reprehensibility in pop:

The shoes on my feet
I bought it
The clothes I'm wearing
I bought it
The rock I'm rockin'
I bought it
'Cause I depend on me
If I wanted the watch you're wearin'
I'll buy it
The house I live in

I bought it
The car I'm driving
I bought it
I depend on me
(I depend on me)

This was the eighties and Madonna's "Material Girl," but multi-
plied a thousand times over and purged of irony. From the
Pussycat Dolls ("Don't you wish your girlfriend was hot like
me") to Lady Gaga ("I want your ugly I want your disease / I
want your everything as long as it's free"), naked mean-spirit-
edness enjoyed a viral ubiquity in mainstream pop. On the other
hand, there was little that was affirmative or aspirational in a
traditional working class "onwards and upwards" sense. With
the notable exception of the Grime/Dubstep sub-continuum – a
localised movement largely confined to certain areas of London
– very few instances of indigenous working class cultural
activity amounted to anything visible in the '00s.

Faced with this emphatic absence of representation, people
resorted in desperation to the celebrities of the new plutocracy
for their folk heroes. Lord Sugar and Baron Lloyd-Webber, who
would have seemed like superannuated relics of a pre-industrial
past even in Dickens's day, attained to a level of credibility they
could only have dreamed about even a few years earlier. A little
further down the scale sat people like Russell Brand, Kate Moss,
Pete Doherty, Jo Whiley, Jonathan Ross, and the Beckhams,
narcissistic new parvenus championing nothing but hedonism
and their own egos, eagerly welcomed into a world of celebrity
and privilege. As with Walliams and Lucas, the persistent notion
that many of these figures were still representatives of alternative culture was perhaps the most damaging aspect of their
elevation to positions of cultural centrality.

A working class hero was no longer something to be, and
when they did emerge, in many cases they acquired the status of

scapegoated social pariahs. The media couldn't quite decide whether Jade Goody was an imbecilic, racist prole, or, as she descended into a gothic spiral of terminal illness and death, a sort of ritualised Marion idol: an unreal, idolised "saint mother" whose demise was played out on the cover of *Hello* magazine and the tabloid newspapers. This was a tragic form of negative celebrity, a peculiarly vindictive form of post-fame *Schadenfreude* which saw hapless (usually working-class) figures finally getting the "comeuppance" their humble origins had always merited. The "white trash" Britney Spears manifested the trend in the U.S., while Paul Gascoigne was another long-running victim of a burgeoning disdain for the lumpen, parochial masses, a perfect caricature of the vulgar, clownish, working class drunk who had somehow gotten lucky. Herein lies part of the pathos of Gazza's apparently misguided implorations that beneath the psycho-pathic exterior, Raoul Moat was really a "good lad." In a misguided but gently demotic, almost untranslatable way, Gazza was trying to combat the sort of hysterical demonization he himself had experienced. He was trying to say that a degree of sympathy should always figure somewhere in our response to the rage of a marginalised madman.

### The Angry Unconscious

In 2010, the director Ridley Scott released a notably terrible film version of the Robin Hood legend. Starring Russell Crowe and Kate Blanchett, the film was a boring, predictably anachronistic vehicle for extended fight scenes, CGI, and barely sentient dialogue, of the kind that has become wearily omnipresent since the release of the first *Lord of the Rings* film in 2001.

However, *Robin Hood* also carried a message that was clearly discernible, if clumsily expressed. In contrast to other recent adaptations of the legend (the Disney version of 1973, 1991's *Robin Hood: Prince of Thieves*), Scott's film went out of its way to exaggerate the latent political connotations in the Hood myth.

Russell Crowe's Robin was not, as in most versions, the dispos-sessed squire Robin of Locksley, who defends the cause of the absent Good King Richard against the cruel, fiscally punitive policies of his brother John. In Scott's version, the benevolent/malign dichotomy within the ruling aristocracy is dispensed with at a very early stage: Richard is killed fighting in France, and henceforth England is ruled exclusively by the tyran-nical John. Meanwhile, Crowe's Robin Longstride, a yeoman archer in the English army, adopts the identity of the murdered knight Robert Locksley. Returning to England, Robin journeys from regal London to Locksley's hometown, a bleakly northern depiction of Nottingham which places a rebellious, starving populace in lieu of the usual Merrie England cliches and Pre-Raphaelite-ish Hollywood pomp. Despite the diversion of a war with a foreign enemy, the really significant divide is between the harshly autocratic King John (a decadently amoral Russell Brand-esque dandy) and Crowe's serious man of the people engineering an insurrectionary Northern rising. The remainder of the film develops this opposition between a corrupt centre and a suffering periphery.

For all the gaucheness and pseudo-mysticism of the film's portrayal of populist revolt (which at one low point is literally reduced to the mawkish slogan "never give up"), there is surely something more significant and timely in its attempt at historical revisionism. Indeed, Scott was arguably tapping into a dormant cultural mentality, an angry, oppositional national unconscious mood that has been covered over by the sort of plutocratic middle-mass hegemony outlined above. That it should take such an ostensibly conservative, mainstream vehicle to give vent to such attitudes is bizarre. Nevertheless, the film's release in May 2010 couldn't have been more apposite. The week that David Cameron entered Downing Street, the highest grossing film in the UK was an avowal of anti-establishment populism, albeit of an incredibly hackneyed kind. Whatever, Cameron might have promised in the way of opposing the Westminster elites, the sort of ordinary folk alluded to in Scott's *Robin Hood* had not really turned out to vote for him in significant numbers in an election that re-emphasised the nation's deep divisions of class, geography, education, and culture. Moreover, as Cameron's hardline anti-sympathy stance became increasingly evident, the divide was likely to become more, rather than less pronounced.

The point is that despite the deleterious developments of the previous thirty years, which seemed to reach a nadir in the radical negativity of the last decade, scattered around the country in small pockets are the remnants of a radically affirmative culture that is founded in collective over individual, sympathetic over unsympathetic, egalitarian over hierarchical values. However, at the moment these characteristics are marginalised to the point that they are finding expression in a host of irrelevant, negative outlets. The sort of suppressed anger that is evident on one hand in atavistic fictional portraits like Ridley Scott's *Robin Hood*, and on the other in horrific and violent media narratives like the Raoul Moat saga, will become increasingly visible in mainstream cultural life over the next few years. The most serious question facing us at this juncture is how to treat such developments.

As the example of America teaches us, full-blown irrationalism and a cult of popular militarism are the obvious dangers resulting from a culture that allows its politics to become a hive of superficial populism and sentimental folksiness. Likewise, countless examples from twentieth century history warn us of the dangers of invoking the people as a mystical salvation. For proof of this we need look no further than the frightening connotations conjured by the German word *Volk*.

Nevertheless, if the British left is to have any sort of future at all, it is to the folk that it must turn, as it always has done. In the past few years it has become easy for even the most liberal voices to sneer at the inarticulate disenfranchised, to partake of a bit of light verbal chav-bashing, to believe the aggressively proffered myth of a progressive and ameliorative classless society. But in the interests of survival, we will have to drop this default attitude of negativity. We will have to seize on the few shreds of solidarity, sympathy, and bottom-up radicalism that are still remaining, and recognise that this is the only heritage we have. In many cases it will simply be a case of throwing the light on areas that have hitherto been kept in the shadows, the sorts of places David Cameron's sympathy would never extend to in a million years.

# 2

# Different Folks

*My music is pastoral. All my songs are based in the English countryside. I never write about London because it doesn't inspire me. I like being here because I meet lots of people, but my heart is in the country. I want to be like Beatrix Potter and move to the Lake District to live with books and plants.*

- Emma-Lee Moss ("Emmy the Great")

## The Opposite of Folk

In October 2010 the BBC hosted a live music event called "Mumford and Sons and Friends" at Cecil Sharp House in North London. The gig was introduced by the hyperbolic Radio 1 DJ Zane Lowe, and the lineup – Mumford and Sons, The Maccabees, Bombay Bicycle Club, Laura Marling – was touted as a celebration of "the new wave of British acoustic artists making a musical impact in 2010." The description of these bands as "British folk-inspired acts" may have been pushing the definition somewhat. Despite their shared interest in twee melodies and faux-colloquial vocals, both The Maccabees and Bombay Bicycle Club were clearly electric, indie-rock oriented acts. Nevertheless, the event was an embodiment of a musical trend that had been burgeoning for some time. This was *nu-folk*, a middlebrow form of pastoral pop, and the BBC's showcase for Mumford and Sons' festival-anthem folk rock was its moment of mainstream apotheosis.

Nu-folk emerged originally out of the American alt-folk and alt-country scenes of the eighties and nineties. By the mid '00s, artists like Joanna Newsom, Grizzly Bear, Bon Iver, and Bill Callahan were at the forefront of a vigorous US-based scene that juxtaposed traditional elements with neo-psychedelic strangeness. Sometimes labeled "acid folk", or "weird folk", the leaders of this sub-genre were typically leftfield experimentalists, eccentric counter-cultural figures embracing the myth of the American frontier. As the US struggled to recapture an affirmative, humane collective identity in the run up to Obama's victory in the 2008 presidential election, this brand of soulful Americana seemed timely and apposite. The Fleet Foxes' eponymous debut album – a fine work of American historical summary, which featured the best use of three-part harmonies by a major band in decades – put a marker on the trend when it was released just a few months before Obama came to power.

The British branch of the genre, however, was a much less exciting proposition. Initially, it looked like there might be a worthwhile renovation of the UK folk heritage. Scottish artists like James Yorkston and King Creosote released a series of innovative, imaginative records in the mid-'00s. Meanwhile, a wider revival of interest in the maverick wing of the '60s/'70s folk revival (The Incredible String Band, Pentangle, Vashti Bunyan) resulted in some interesting local activity in places like Fife and Chorlton/Didsbury in Manchester. Aging DJs swapped techno and hip-hop records for obscure psychedelic folk rock. In London, Kieran Hebden (aka Four Tet) was a key figure in the birth of folktronica, an intriguing, if sometimes uninspiring sub-genre.

However, by the time of the Zane Lowe gig at Cecil Sharp House in late 2010, the coffee-table commercialism of Mumford and Sons (and associated artists like Emmy the Great, Laura Marling, Noah and the Whale, and Johnny Flynn) had become the dominant tendency in UK nu-folk. Unfortunately, this slick, bankable trend, described by Lowe as a "new wave of acoustic artists," had far more in common with MOR singer-songwriters like Jack Johnson and Kate Nash than it did with counter-cultural forerunners like Bert Jansch and Fairport Convention. Musically pedestrian to the point of utter banality, and lacking either a firm grasp of tradition or any experimental impulse whatsoever, genre-defining songs like "5 Years Time" by Noah and the Whale and "The Cave" by Mumford and Sons were travesties of the notion of newness, corporate pastiches of a traditional aesthetic.

But one of the most notable things about the nu-folk ascendancy was its social makeup. Interestingly, almost every single member of the Mumford and Sons and Friends lineup was educated at a private fee-paying school in London or the surrounding area (and the same 4 or 5 schools at that). We are all used to having to allow for the disproportionate influence of private-school alumni in British society, but not, perhaps, in pop music, and certainly not to this emphatic extent[9]. A private education is an unfortunate psychic handicap for any individual; we should be wary of cruel inverse snobbery and try to avoid clumsy moralism by judging each person on his or her own case. But this is not a question of individual ethics. Rather, a structural trend like this should interest us because it shows just how much the makeup of pop music has been transformed in recent times.

Whatever the new sub-genre led by Mumford and Sons and Friends denoted, it could scarcely be described as folk in the sense of an ordinary, grassroots populace. In fact, this musical phenomenon was an appropriation of the onetime art of the rural and urban proletariat by a privileged, youthful mandarin caste. When it was claimed that Laura Marling was a descendant of William the Conqueror, most people looked on this as a charming but irrelevant piece of biographical information. Yet the symbolic connection of a modern metropolitan elite to an ancient aristocracy was unfortunately all too apt. At the start of the 2010s, British culture was presided over by a social demographic bolstered by inherited power and influence in a way not seen since the Second World War, and nu-folk was the music of choice for this new elite.

How did this inversion of folk culture's raison d'être occur?

As egalitarianism and social mobility began to fall by the wayside in the '90s and '00s, there were signs that the old British class system was creeping back with a vengeance after the populist, reformist tides of the post-war period. But the spectacular co-option of the accoutrements of populist art, old and new, by an affluent upper-middle class that accompanied the return of a stratified social order was an interesting twist. Why did this new plutocracy seize so eagerly on nu-folk pop music as a means of culturally defining itself, and what sort of worldview was being affirmed by this consumer fantasy of bucolic populism?

## The Cultural Logic of Green Toryism

One of David Cameron's stabs at "progressivism" in the run-up to the 2010 election, one of his most blatant attempts to win over the new plutocratic liberal centre, was the projection of the Green Conservative PR myth. In a much-hyped 2008 speech, Cameron performed an act of cartoon rebranding when he declared that green should join blue as one of the primary colours of Conservative Party identity. The old Tory logo (a blue torch) was swapped for a badly drawn English oak tree, an emblem that tapped into both Tory traditionalism and the new plutocracy's hankering after a kooky rural lifestyle. In reality, what looked like an attempt to innovate a European-style progressive conservatism was little more than an ad-hoc piece of image-making, a publicity stunt that was forgotten after a minor media kerfuffle. A party as dedicated to economic sadism as Cameron's New Tories was never going to possess either the wherewithal or the means to embark on even a modest programme of public spending directed at environmentalist reform. The actual British Green Party won their first ever parliamentary seat in 2010, in Brighton and Hove, on a mandate of decidedly anti-Tory left-liberalism, and any prospect of a meaningful Conservative capturing of the Green ethos seemed to have evaporated.

Nevertheless, for all that the new Green Toryism was an

obviously spurious gimmick, it was a pithy and accurate summation of the British middle-class zeitgeist at the turn of the decade. Specifically, its relevance lay in its metaphorical synthesis of Old Tory myths of organic order with the values of a new hegemonic bourgeois class, one that was yearning for a cultural paradigm that would simultaneously justify its escapist lifestyle and its often unconscious dedication to hierarchy and inheritance.

The mood and values of Green Toryism were so pervasive that it defined even the cultural outlook of many non-Tory voters, garnering sympathy from the class that had sustained and profited from Blairism – *Guardianistas*, Nick Clegg acolytes, the new legions of allotment keepers, aging indie musicians – as well as from the Old and New Right base that was by definition always inclined towards aristocratic and pseudo-aristocratic values. Its shibboleths were littered across the culture. Hugh Fearnley-Whittingstall's *River Cottage* franchise was one of the runaway TV success stories of the late '00s, so much so that by the beginning of the new decade its presenter had the temerity to venture into working-class council homes to lecture the beleaguered inhabitants on the virtues of organic eating. Barbour jackets became frighteningly ubiquitous. Lily Allen, a privately educated London popstar with famous entertainment industry parents left the music business after meteoric success and celebrity to live with her ducks and run a small clothing business in the Surrey countryside[10]. *Tamara Drewe*, the film version of Posy Simmonds's comic-strip Thomas Hardy homage, was a Richard Curtis-like daydream picture that secured the link between the modern liberal bourgeoisie and an older English literary tradition of pastoralism, painting a picture of idealised rural permanence. Overall, the classic popular cultural depiction of the countryside was as a quasi-fictional playground for London professionals indulging in weekend escapism.

In intellectual circles, eco-criticism became one of the most successful academic brands of the age. This was an often vital and necessary attempt to combine cultural analysis with environmental activism, of which there are countless positive examples. Yet eco-crit could also be expressive of a liberal elite that was shockingly unaware of the connection between its pseudo-green worldview and the aloof, fantastical existence it was leading. One of the most prominent eco-critics, the biographer and minor literary celebrity Jonathan Bate, published a newspaper article-cum-property ad in the *Telegraph* newspaper in late-2010 that garnered notoriety for being a revealing expose of the mindset of the author of *Romantic Ecology* and *Song of the Earth*. Bate lamented the fact that he had been offered the mastership of Worcester College, Oxford, because accepting would mean selling both his St. Tropez apartment and his Queen Anne farmhouse in rural Warwickshire. Part of the tragedy was that the Warwickshire house had been the setting for a delightful pastoral idyll as described by Bate, one in which his wife researched her Jane Austen biography by absorbing village gossip, and in which his daughter was crowned the "May Queen" in the midst of exquisitely quaint springtime festivities.

As with the corporate-trad of Mumford and Sons and their ilk, these avowals of folksiness and green identity were part of a top-down inversion of the notion of an indigenous grassroots. The more the British middle-class benefited from an ultra-modern, ultra-technological system of global production, the more they sought refuge in a cult of the earth that suggested they were still in sympathetic allegiance with a humble, peasant-like way of life. As Cameron's New Tories began to implement the most profoundly un-sympathetic, anti-populist agenda in living memory, there was solace in the mirage of an eternal, agrarian world that would safeguard earthiness, simplicity, quasi-pagan mythology, and primitive labour no matter how viciously actual working class people were treated by a neoliberal economy founded on minority (urban) affluence.

As is so often the case with unequal power dynamics, inequality was compounded by that fact that the dominant influence managed to seize the garments and vocabulary of the opposing side. In place of a real engagement with a modern day proletariat, Green Toryism propounded the fiction of a sturdy rural yeomanry dedicated to service, on hand to provide labour for upper-middle-class consumer whims like real ale and organic food. In a very literal sense, the folk became the property of the anti-folk, who were then able to characterise the identity of "the people" in whatever way they saw fit. Without significant opposition, a hierarchy comprising old Tories and a new upper-bourgeois caste was utterly free to develop and consolidate its inordinate wealth and centrality, while the real folk populace languished behind an all-encompassing wall of silence.

## Some Versions of Pastoral

The alliance between old Tory interests and an arriviste new plutocracy was a far from novel development; certainly, the fluid relationship between these two groups has been a perennial fixture of British social history. Similarly, the enthusiastic endorsement of pastoral myths by the upper echelons of the British class system is a tendency that can be traced at least as far back as first generation Romanticism, that is, to the beginnings of modern liberalism, and to the first signs of a reactive response that would begin as a corrective to laissez-faire capitalism, but end up as an essential concomitant of it. This narrative took place at the same time as modern conservatism completed its long transition from being exclusively the party of landed gentry, to being a flexible, inclusive ideological nexus for whichever privileged, elite interests were thrown up in the march of liberal capitalist orthodoxy. For this tendency, the pastoral ideal provided an ersatz conservatism, a mythic aristocratic heritage that could be purchased easily by anyone rich enough to rub shoulders with the ruling ascendancy.

Very broadly speaking, we might say that there have always been two strands of British Romantic culture, two opposing traditions that have remained separate and antithetical despite a number of ostensible similarities and occasional moments of intersection. On the one hand is the radically egalitarian and pantheistic tendency that provided the original impetus for the emergence of British Romanticism in the late-eighteenth century. Outright radicals like Thomas Paine, William Blake, and Thomas Bewick belong obviously in this lineage, but arguably so too does a work like Wordsworth's and Coleridge's *Lyrical Ballads*, with its polemical advocacy of ordinary speech, its deistic leanings, and its energetic revival of the popular ballad form. In an important sense, the modern view of folk culture as an empowering spiritual and political force begins here, with these Romantic attempts to critique an acquisitive capitalistic culture by avowing diverse forms of populism (the ballad, the engraving, the political pamphlet, egalitarian thought).

Throughout the nineteenth century this strain of radical Romanticism provided the basis for the development of class-consciousness amongst the rural and urban proletariat, and for the rise of socialism as a meaningful socio-cultural phenomenon. Like their first generation Romantic predecessors, figures such as Robert Owen and William Morris drew on a pastoral ideal when formulating their utopian socialist schemes. In the radical tradition the countryside was less a chimerical fantasy than a real place where theories about collective living and autonomous craftsmanship could be tested out. A few miles down the road from David Cameron's current constituency of Witney, C.R. Ashbee established an artistic commune in the Cotswold town of Chipping Camden in the last years of the nineteenth century. A key influence on the foundation of the proto-modernist German *Werkbund* movement from which the Bauhaus arose, Ashbee's experiment in rural living is an example of a radical Romantic tradition based on socialist praxis, one that ultimately fed into and galvanised the progressive mainstream of modern European art.

Clearly, this version of pastoralism was far from hermetic and disengaged. Although for Ashbee, Morris and many other utopian socialists, the pastoral was an embodiment of an anti-industrial medievalism that was markedly, even consciously mythologised and nostalgic, this tendency also existed alongside a serious examination and analysis of working practices, and a forward-thinking emphasis on collectivism and innovative design that would subsequently be adopted by twentieth century political and artistic movements on both sides of the rural-urban divide. This wing of British Romanticism showed a clear bias for the country over the town; however, in focusing on real people and actual craftsmanship, it also avoided the trap of viewing the pastoral as a vague receptacle of mythic truth and beauty. Above all, this was a populist Romanticism that could align itself with the causes of the urban as well as the rural poor, with artisans and a unionised proletariat as well as with a diminishing rural labouring class. In short, this cultural mode was one of the main forms of expression for a British folk that was just beginning to be aware of itself.

## The Conservative Elegiac Tradition

Of course, this radical strain has always been at odds with what we might term the conservative elegiac tradition of British Romanticism. Wordsworth's trajectory from youthful radical to disillusioned Tory tree-hugger is a famous instance of oscillation between the two strands, and along with figures like Burke and Coleridge, he is one of the main originators of the modern reactionary tendency to view the pastoral world as both an impregnable bastion of organic order and a place of leisurely retreat. In this tradition, the pastoral was both a paradigm for the feudal world that had been left behind in the march towards industrialization, and an expression of middle-class aspiration towards a neo-feudal ideal. Queen Victoria, the "middle-class queen" and icon of the age, was a perfect summation of this Establishment Romanticism, with her fondness for sentimental ballads, and her enthusiasm for the Scottish Highlands as filtered through the aristocratic-medievalist imagination of Sir Walter Scott. As the eighteenth century ideal of the fashionable urban townscape gave way to a valorization of suburban living and rural leisure pursuits in the Victorian era, this version of the pastoral was a means of solidifying the link between the old aristocracy and the nouveau riche. The notion of the Englishman's home as a castle, with the obligatory country garden attached, encapsulates this sense of a pseudo-royal lifestyle mythos that was, allegedly, available to everyone.

On the eve of the outbreak of modernism in the first decades of the twentieth century, bourgeois pastoralism was at its height. This was the era in which the public-school-educated Cecil Sharp would compile an exhaustive survey of English folk music, a project that has since been viewed with profound ambivalence. In many ways a valuable ethnographic project, Sharp's *English Folk Songs* was also a classic instance of the upper-middle-class misappropriation of popular art forms, an endeavour founded in Sharp's elegiac romantic sense that the "peasantry" were the guardians of a rural heritage in imminent danger of extinction. Perhaps unsurprisingly, urban ballads were largely excluded from this supposedly comprehensive anthology of working class music, a reflection of the skewed, selective nature of Sharp's patronage of folk culture. Sharp's pre-First World War contemporaries like Ralph Vaughan Williams and the Georgian school of poets (A.E. Housman, Robert Bridges, Edward Thomas) shared Sharp's basic standpoint: the countryside was a place to be raided for its aesthetic resources, or else a place for an increasingly insecure late-Imperialist ascendancy to wallow in nostalgia and melancholia.

While the First World War is often seen as having put a stop to this obsession with bucolic traditionalism, there were numerous reiterations of it in the ensuing decades. F.R. Leavis's work in establishing English literature a serious subject for higher educational study was in part founded on the elegiac Romantic yearning for a return to organic unity; so too was the related academic school of New Criticism, as well as a certain strain in the novels and essays of D.H. Lawrence that would be co-opted by Leavis as an artistic adjunct to his organicist theories. But as Britain inched ever closer to the egalitarian moment of the post-war period, there was a definite falling off of this variety of pastoralism. Published in the late-1940s, Evelyn Waugh's *Brideshead Revisited* represented a sort of last gasp of the elegiac tradition. The novel's opening section, with its Virgilian title *Et in Arcadia Ego* ("I [death] am also in Arcadia") and its vast nostalgia for an obsolescent aristocratic existence, was symptomatic of a prevailing sense during this period that the traditional order was not only on the wane, but about to be comprehensively dismantled in a world of universal suffrage and the Welfare State.

## Folk Revival: Towards a Modernist Pastoral

The post-war years were the occasion for a massive culture-wide revival of the radical Romantic tradition initiated by Bewick, Blake, Morris and others in the late-eighteenth and nineteenth centuries, an event that coincided with the rise of the New Left and the emergence of a counter-culture in Europe and North America. As with much post-war cultural activity, the seeds of the folk revival had been sown in the twenties and thirties; we might point to the Right to Roam movement and the foundation of the Jean-Jacques Rousseau-esque Woodcraft Folk youth organisation in the interwar years, as two key preemptive developments. But from the late-fifties onwards, this version of pastoralism – one that was inextricably bound up with mid-twentieth century radical politics – would come to occupy an increasingly central position in the post-war imagination. The popular folk culture of the period was reflective of a moment of profound populism, the artistic and intellectual fallout from social contexts such as the great expansion of higher education, the rise of mass media and new technologies as disseminators of popular art, and of course the basic fact that, in Britain at least, the folk now had control of the state and cultural apparatus in a way that had been unimaginable prior to this point.

The revival of folk music led the way in foregrounding a pastoralism that was popular and modernistic rather than nostalgic and aristocratic. Revivalists like A.L. Lloyd and Ewan MacColl differed markedly from Cecil Sharp in their attempts at re-popularising the folksong, partly because they did not share Sharp's over-idealised view of rurality. Industrial ballads were integral to the post-war folk revival, and much of its activity took place in cities: in urban folk clubs like the Ballad and Blues in Soho, as well as in countryside festivals and small-town "gatherings." The overwhelmingly socialistic, modern, progressive orientation of the revival obviated any arbitrary distinctions between the town and the country. Moreover, this folk culture had a healthy respect for technology: recorded sound was key to the preservation and continuation of the movement. The revival may have been subject to a streak of puritanism, of which the most notable instance was probably the pillorying of Bob Dylan on a 1965 British tour for his abandonment of purebred folk for a new electric sound. But overall the luddite tendency was a marginal one.

Just as its view of the town-country divide was distinctly fluid, post-war folk culture was, on the whole, open to formal experimentation and generic expansion: this was no mere dualistic alternative to modern industrial pop music. As the sixties progressed, the pastoral became a leitmotif of the burgeoning counter-culture, and was subject to hybridization and a variety of radical re-appropriations. Folk's galvanizing relationship with counter-cultural rock resulted in some of the finest music in pop history, from outright folk rock (Dylan, The Byrds, The Band, Fairport Convention) to that obscure strain of psychedelic folk that has enjoyed such an enthusiastic revival in the first decade of the twenty-first century (of which the most famous representatives were perhaps Pentangle and The Incredible String Band).

Whether it was acting as inspiration for the nascent environmental movement, or as a justification for neo-Owenite hippy communes, or as an offshoot of a union culture entering its twilight years, the form of folk-pastoral that dominated the post-war decades was a progressive force in an age dominated by a broadly egalitarian ethos. It is difficult for us to look beyond the clichés that have characterised this period and its artworks since a climate of retro-consumerism took hold in the eighties and nineties. If we think of the 1960s and folk music, we think of consumer accoutrements, of woolly jumpers, Martin acoustic guitars, and beards[11]. Or perhaps we think of the 2005 mockumentary *Mighty is the Wind* (essentially *Spinal Tap II*), Christopher Guest's brilliant parody of sixties folk-rock. What such perspectives must not obscure is that counter-cultural pastoralism began as a politically motivated, basically forward-looking movement that aligned a traditional heritage with a dedication to subversion and the shock of the new. At bottom, it was the cultural consequence of a social demographic that was attaining to a new, modern form of enfranchisement, at the same time as it was still intimately connected to its disenfranchised, communitarian roots. This was the artistic medium of the sons and daughters of an empowered folk for whom a basic belief in collectivism still triumphed over self-regard and individualism.

## Brideshead Resurrected

Perhaps the first signs of a return to a version of pastoralism founded in nostalgia and wealth-fantasy came with the hugely popular ITV dramatisation of Waugh's *Brideshead* in 1981, right at the start of the Thatcher era. But it would take much longer for this symptom of Thatcherite neoliberalism to achieve centrality in the mainstream of British culture. "Thatcher's children" is an epithet often applied to the young adults of the eighties and nineties, to the first generation of school leavers and twentysome-things who either embraced an ideal of money and self-reliance or else had to face the consequences of high unemployment and a climate of unchecked acquisitiveness. Actually, the phrase would be far better used as a way of describing the real children of that long decade, those born between 1979 and 1990 under Thatcher's premiership, a generation that has only very recently attained to social maturity and influence[12]. For an example of the cultural outlook of a certain privileged wing of these real Children of Thatcher, we might look to the "This Side of Paradise" Ball of July 2011, at St John's College, Oxford. In publicity released within days of the student demonstrations against the three-fold rise in tuition fees, this £175 event was advertised as an attempt to "invoke the style and sophistication of a more elegant era." The organisers went on to state:

> ...it is our opinion that the standard of balls in Oxford has been dropping for some time, and we hope to revive the Oxford Ball in all its glory. With this in mind, we would like to bring you back into the world of Wodehouse and Waugh, and to show you a college transformed.

For a long time it was the urbanite, Blairite strain of neo-liberalism that presided in British culture (witness the "cockney" and "manc" archetypes of '90s Britpop, and the Dickensian-ruffian aesthetic of early '00s bands like The Libertines and Razorlight). But as the St John's "This Side of Paradise" Ball underlines, by the beginning of the 2010s, with a new ultra-Thatcherite government in power, the aristocratic pastoralism that Waugh had eulogised back in 1948 in *Brideshead Revisited* was back with a vengeance. The conservative elegiac tradition had somehow come to rule British cultural life once again.

The congregation of a new, unashamedly wealthy demographic behind Green Toryism and its musical cousin nu-folk was perhaps inevitable. Without restraining influences, British elites will probably always return to pastoral myth as a means of hiding inequality under a carapace of fairytale, neo-feudal commonality. An unfortunate development though was the incorporation of the surface features of radical post-war counter-cultural folk into the mythos[13]. As in countless other instances over the last few decades, the possibility of a real alternative culture, of a real popular opposition to neoliberal hegemony, has been stifled by a casual, consumerist appropriation of the subversive art of previous epochs. As Thatcher and her political successors have progressively remodeled Britain so that it is a country in which ancient interests share power with the profiteers of liberal aspirationalism, we have seen a return to the pre-twentieth century arrangement whereby the country is ruled by an elite which divides its time between a practice of wealth generation in the city, and an identity founded in the countryside where it spends its leisure time. At the start of the 2010s, the cultural mainstream is overwhelmingly dominated by a newly confident upper-middle-class, one that has a formidable monopoly on the contemporary sense of what "alternative culture" means. In music, as across an entire culture, the heirs of William the Conqueror are wearing the folk's clothing.

# 3

# Oppositional Geography

*How do you get from here to the rest of the world?*

*- Dukie, The Wire.*

## The North-East of England as a Quidditch Pitch

The Duke of Northumberland's Alnwick Castle residence was one of the great tourist success stories of the last decade. At the turn of the century, the Duke's wife Jane Northumberland initiated the Alnwick Garden project, a lottery-funded attempt to build the most ambitious new garden created in Britain since the Second World War. The original garden was designed by Capability Brown in the mid-eighteenth century; over the next two hundred years it underwent a series of lavish renovations. In the Victorian period, the fourth Duke introduced an Italianate garden complete with wrought iron Venetian gates, and by the end of the nineteenth century, as a potted history on the official website informs us the gardens were "at their grandest with yew topiary, avenues of limes and acres of flowers." However, after this late-imperial high-watermark, the Duke's estate experienced moderate decline; when WWII struck, the garden was co-opted by the British state to function as a vegetable plot in the Dig For Victory campaign. Thereafter, as the official website laments, "the austerity of the twentieth century saw the garden fall into disrepair."

Happily, by the beginning of the twenty-first century, the Duke and Duchess were able to capitalise on a new climate of prosperity. The Duchy provided the 42-acre site and £9 million towards construction costs, but the remainder of the £42 million budget was bolstered by lottery grants and charitable donations.

Ancient and modern forms of money generation were allied: the Duke and Duchess were able to revive the fortunes of their estate and its environs, and to pull off a remarkable public relations coup in the process. After the site opened to the public in 2001, it quickly became the third most-visited paid entry garden in the country after Kew and Wisley. Boosted by a starring role in the first Harry Potter film, in which it provided the setting for the quidditch match, the ancestral seat of the Percy family became an icon of renewed affluence that mirrored a region-wide revival[14]. In the noughties, the north-east of England ("Northumbria" in tourist industry parlance) became an amiable leisure destination, and Alnwick Castle was one of its most auspicious showpieces.

The regeneration of Alnwick Castle – a project that combined public and private investment to revive a notoriously neglected part of the country - was a classic example of New Labour cultural mission in action. Indeed, the north-east as a whole was one of the key power bases of the New Labour project, partly because so many of the party's top echelon had parliamentary seats in the region. Nearly all of the most prominent architects of Blairism were north-east MPs (Mandelson, Milburn, David Miliband, and Blair himself) although most of these figures largely abandoned their ties to the area after the 1997 election victory[15]. But even though its political representatives eventually migrated southward to establish the headquarters of Cool Britannia in the capital, the glamour of the early years of Blairism lingered on in the north-east for some time. To borrow a slogan of NewcastleGateshead's unsuccessful 2008 European Capital of Culture bid, the north-east was "buzzin'" for most of the noughties[16]. Just as champagne socialism defined the New Labour zeitgeist, a champagne Geordie mentality prevailed in this almost exclusively Labour-voting enclave[17]. The former industrial wasteland that was the quayside area of the city underwent a lively regeneration. A coolly minimalist sixth bridge across the Tyne (The Millenium), a Tate Modern-like art gallery

(The Baltic), and an insectoid Sir Norman Foster-designed concert hall (The Sage) completed a trio of sparkling nouveau developments in the heart of Tyneside's old shipbuilding district. Geordie nightlife became legendary in an era of hard-drinking hedonism and bar culture. To top it all, local lads Ant and Dec became the nation's favourite TV presenters. In many ways, it seemed as though things really had gotten better for the Geordie nation.

Many of these developments were a source of genuine enthusiasm and pride for a large number of north-easterners during this period. For all that New Labour to a large extent continued the work begun by the Thatcher in the 1980s, in the north-east the passage from Thatcherism to Blairism was marked by a subtle shift in atmosphere. The transformation of the region from a thoroughly depressed epicentre of the miners' strike to a lively showcase of millennial culture had a tangible positive effect; few living in the area in the early years of the twenty-first century could escape the pervasive mood of civic confidence engendered by the redevelopments.

Yet there was another side to the champagne Geordie miracle. The regeneration of the Newcastle and Gateshead quayside areas may have been symbolically effective from the point of view of morale, but in the long-term, New Labour's regeneration of the region amounted to little more than wafer-thin symbolism. By the end of the 2010s, nothing much had changed for the majority of north-easterners. They now had some expensive venues in which to listen to classical music and gaze at contemporary art, and there were some wonderful new tourist attractions in Northumberland to visit at weekends (one of which had provided the backdrop for an inordinately popular Hollywood film franchise). But aside from these largely upper-middle-class leisure tokens, real regeneration of this post-industrial Labour heartland was conspicuously lacking. Unemployment was still high, health still poor, and mainstream cultural representation still ambivalent at best. Most of the region's jobs were in the public sector, so when state spending was slashed in the last days of New Labour and decimated in the first days of Cameron's coalition government, there was creeping realisation that the cultural revival of the '00s had been little more than an elaborate piece of Blairite spin. The north-east may have enjoyed a period of cosmetic growth in the years after 1997, but when the tide of affluence went out, the short-lived renaissance of the early twentieth century left relatively little behind. A lasting social or economic infrastructure was certainly not one of the legacies of cultural regeneration, and things were still pretty grim in this part of the north, even if the entertainment industry could now portray it as a hyperreal CGI terrain in films that glorified English public school culture. Alnwick Castle (and its quidditch pitch) was still flourishing, but this was less a symbol of prosperity than a token that neoliberal consumer culture had completed a successful conquest of the north-east. Only really in the realms of neo-aristocratic Hollywood fantasy was this a good time to be a Northumbrian.

## Alternative Space

You can tell there is something meaningful and potentially subversive in a concept when it is tamed and reduced to a coffee-table cliché by the London media and publishing industries. In the noughties, this is what happened with the notion of a north-south divide. Books like Stuart Maconie's *Pies and Prejudice,* Judith Holder's *It's (Not) Grim Up North,* and Martin Wainwright's *True North* were intelligent and well-meaning dissections of northern culture, but they were positioned in a critical space that was never going to allow for the germ of a serious argument to grow. Instead of provoking debate about real regional differences based on solid economic, political, and historical factors, the culture industry subsumed the north-south debate into fashionable analyses of "Englishness"[18]. As the

English tried to establish an affirmative sense of self in a liberal, post-Imperial world, depoliticised discussions of place and identity became newly popular. Hence, if the north was not being subjected to nineteenth century caricatures in comedy shows like *Little Britain* and *Phoenix Nights*[19] it fell victim to the middlebrow valorisation of "the local." Polite psycho-geography papered over potential devolutionary schisms, and watered-down, commercial stereotypes of regionalism became de rigeur.

In the north of England, life expectancies and salaries are lower, jobs and educational opportunities are fewer, health is poorer, and lifestyles are markedly less comfortable than in most parts of the south. Statistics demonstrating these trends will be familiar to everyone: they are an accepted facet of socio-economic discourse. Yet while the statistical basis of the north-south divide is rarely disputed, there persists a sense that categorical distinctions between northern and southern England are somehow chauvinistic. For both the conservative unionist and the *bien pensant* liberal, sweeping geographical generalisations are seen as the remnants of an anachronistic tribalism, and regionalist theories should be treated with fierce scepticism. In conservative eyes, the north is a vulgar periphery or, alternatively, a mountainous idylll and loyal tributary of the Crown. Meanwhile, according to modern liberal doctrine, there can be no one north, only a plurality of "norths." It would be reductive to overlook diversity and individual difference in the service of a totalising narrative. According to this view, the twentieth century showed us the dangers of mystified projections of group identity, and we must avoid repeating such mistakes at all costs.

Taken together, these viewpoints represent a formidable modern consensus behind the idea that regional sentiment simply no longer exists (if, indeed, it ever did). To argue to the contrary would be a sentimental indulgence at best, a pseudo-racialising travesty at worst. Yet the example of the north-east, at least, would appear to contradict this thesis. "Geordie nationalism" is a powerful force in the region. Newcastle is famously a one-club footballing city, and its team, Newcastle United, is the conduit of a fiercely autonomous regional identity. Separated from the rest of the country by the Pennines and the dales and moors of North Yorkshire, the north-east retains the feel of an island-like locality. St George's flags and England replica shirts, ubiquitous even in the north-west, are replaced in this part of the country by Newcastle United and Sunderland paraphernalia; Union Jacks are not often seen; the region's accents are distinctive to the point of inimitability. Despite the inroads made by New Labour's cultural initiatives, gentrification has been relatively limited in this part of the country, perhaps because it is so far out of commuting distance from any of the UK's major financial and business centres: there is no substantial "stockbroker belt." The wealth gap is much less pronounced in this area than in most southern cities, and class divisions are much less emphatic[20].

In short, the north-east is an idiosyncratic place, perhaps the polar opposite of a London that has enthusiastically reactivated its status as an imperial centre over the last thirty years of neoliberal hegemony. If we are going to take geography seriously as a shaper of social status and cultural identity – and there is surely a case for doing so – we must try to delineate the nature of this opposition between capital and periphery. Is England a place of relative egalitarianism across its regions? Is the contemporary cross-party commitment to "fairness" evidence of a consensus behind an equable, proportional distribution of wealth, power, and influence in all of the nation's localities? This is clearly not the case, and in fact such enforced equality would amount to a total repudiation of neoliberal doctrine, which is at bottom in favour of letting prosperity develop unimpeded wherever chance dictates. Unquestionably, deep-seated inequalities continue to cast long, jagged shadows over the map of England. Yet there is still a sense, from both liberals and conservatives, that these imbalances do not exist or should not be acted on, that basically *things are the same everywhere.* What is being held in check by this denial of difference between England's metropolitan centre and its regional margins? If we can agree that there is an inordinate concentration of power in London and its environs, and that this has led to all manner of negative developments, might there not be great potential in taking geographical difference very seriously indeed? Isn't an independently minded north-east one of the main places we should look to if we are trying to find an oppositional alternative to a conservative ascendancy that is now often explicit in declaring partisan loyalty to its southern heart-lands?

## Oppositional Precedent No. 1: Breaking the Power Structure

Pro-regional sentiment is as old as Northumbria itself, of course. But it seemed to reach a kind of apogee in the mid-twentieth century in a period of popular enfranchisement and expanding egalitarianism. In the north-east, two figures in particular are notable for their compelling articulations of the case for greater regional autonomy. One is a cautionary tale, the other a relatively little-known entity, an example of a more affirmative form of Northumbrian identity.

The first figure is T. Dan Smith, the charismatic but infamous leader of Newcastle City Council from 1960 to 1965. Smith was born in Wallsend, Tyneside in 1915 into a mining family with Communist sympathies. During World War II he was a conscientious objector, but became a supporter of the war effort after the German invasion of the Soviet Union in 1941. Then, in the immediate post-war period, Smith joined the Labour Party, and from this moment onward his future lay in politics.

Smith's early-sixties tenure as council leader was the occasion for a massive regeneration of Newcastle, the effects of which are still evident fifty years later. Dedicated to creating a "Brasilia of the North," Smith embarked on a substantial slum clearance programme, which was combined with a building scheme that saw vigorous modernist developments spring up all across the city[21]. Newcastle became the first English city to have a planning department. Its activities led to ambitious architectural projects such as Ryder and Yates' MEA House, Basil Spence's Central Library, and a series of vertiginous, futuristic walkways designed by the Scottish architectural firm Robert Matthew-John Marshall; there were also proposals for a shopping centre to be designed by Scandinavian modernist heavyweight Arne Jacobson, and another (ultimately unrealised) plan to persuade Le Corbusier to choose Newcastle as the location for his first building project in the UK. Smith's ambition to create a northern powerhouse city resulted in the creation of the buildings that would eventually house Newcastle Polytechnic (now Northumbria University) and to the first proposals for a metro train system (which finally opened in 1980, and is still functioning successfully). He was also responsible for the foundation of the Northern Arts Association. In other words, much of the civic infrastructure that exists to this day in the north-east was in some way a result of the actions of Smith and his Labour council.

One interesting element in Smith's utopian project was the emphasis on drawing out the distinctive sense of place in Newcastle. For all that the architectural developments came to be seen as egregious eyesores, there was something aptly Novocastrian about these bold, industrial constructions. Brash, monolithic, and appropriately black and white, the new buildings captured the spirit of a city that had long sought to declare its nonconformity with English stereotypes through a commitment to internationalism, bravura modernity, and audacity in the arts. However, this was not merely a question of aesthetics. Smith's attempt to emphasise Newcastle's unique identity was underwritten by a staunch anti-establishment sensibility that also found expression in concrete schemes for regional devolution. In order to counteract the dominance of what he termed the "power structure" (that "mighty, non-elected, all-powerful group of people", as he put it) Smith argued that the House of Lords should be replaced by a body of regional representatives, who would be elected to serve the interests of eleven localised sub-divisions (Smith would at other times advocate a five-province devolution scheme, with a northern "capital" based in Manchester). As Smith argued in a late-1980s TV interview,

> ...[once an elected regional second chamber is created] you begin to break the power of that group of invisible men and women who you see in the *Times* court circular every day; and the ridiculous farcical titles that they hang on to and clutch, while they tell the working people "you've got to move with the times – you've got to be prepared to give up your craft and your job." They give up nothing, even the ridiculous titles they give themselves.

For Smith, delegating power to the regions of England through a comprehensive devolutionary programme was a key precondition of an egalitarian society. In his view, the English power dynamic is inherently geographical; divisions of place are one of the pre-eminent means by which economic disparities are perpetuated and power concentrated in the hands of a privileged minority. A system based on strong, energetic regional provinces facing outwards to Europe and the rest of the world is one of the major ways of counteracting the structural inequalities of British society.

Smith's democratic, republican version of folk opposition was in many ways a rational, persuasive one. Yet, as the caustic, ranting tone in the above quotation indicates, he was also a somewhat embittered figure whose personal weaknesses left him open to the usual charges leveled at populist regionalism: those of bias, chauvinism, sectarianism, and, most critically in Smith's case, egotism. Smith's self-regard and belief in his own myth was his undoing. By the time of the late-'80s TV interviews he was an isolated, easily dismissible desperado, the kind you might expect to make sweeping paranoid statements alluding to a sinister cabal of London-based powerbrokers. In Smith's skewed view, it was this power network that was responsible for his spectacular fall from grace in the 1970s. Accusations of corruption led to a series of trials, of which the upshot was that Smith had sought to profit personally from the Newcastle regeneration projects in the early sixties. His construction firm had received an inordinate proportion of building commissions, and Smith had also been involved in a number of shady dealings with John Poulson, a property developer who was convicted for nefarious activities all across the north. Smith suffered the same fate as Poulson when he received a six-year prison sentence in 1974, after pleading guilty to charges of corruption in a London court. By this point, the spirit of hyperborean expansionism that Smith had helped to fuel in early-sixties Newcastle was beginning to wane; just around the corner, the Thatcher era would provide the occasion for its utter repudiation.

## Oppositional Precedent No. 2: Basil Bunting's Northern Rising

On the margins of a culture the gap between outlaw and luminary can be slight. Maybe all northern champions are ultimately destined to play the role of the embattled, quixotic outsider. But they do not all succumb to outright criminality like T. Dan Smith. With the flick of a switch oppositional sentiment can become a soulful, progressive raison d'être.

One of the beneficiaries of the Northern Arts organisation founded by Smith was the veteran modernist poet Basil Bunting, who became its president in 1974. Ironically, just a few months prior to Bunting's appointment, a Regional Director of Northern Arts had stated, "Northumberland is dead, and its so-called folk-culture. So are the pits." His allegiances were starkly proclaimed: "I am from the Home Counties", he stated, "I regard my mission as bringing arts to the North." This priceless archetype of southern imperiousness was one that Bunting had spent his whole life kicking against, as he sought to arrive at a poetic philosophy that treated northern English identity and radical modernism as one and the same thing. As the critic Peter Quartermain has commented:

> Bunting's position as a writer of English poetry in [the twentieth] century has been notably marginal, and, I believe, deliberately so. It is part and parcel not only of his identification of himself as a Northumbrian writer, but also of his deliberate and conscious determination to be a *modern* writer[22].

The version of Northumbrian modernism that Bunting was able to put into practice in the sixties and seventies – partly on the foundation of Dan Smith's civic enterprises – is an example of what happens when a genuinely progressive, anti-establishment local culture is given the space to breathe.

Born in 1900 in Scotswood-on-Tyne, Bunting was brought up in a Quaker household and this non-conformist background laid the foundations of a lifelong aversion to what Smith might have called the English power structure. After a deeply unhappy spell at a southern boarding school as a teenager, Bunting was imprisoned as a conscientious objector in the final months of the First World War. His experience of being beaten, stripped naked, and kept in solitary confinement – a typical treatment for "conchies" at this time – was one that would resonate throughout the remainder of his life. Bunting's opposition to the English establishment cut right to the bone.

In the 1920s Bunting studied briefly at the London School of Economics before finding work as a secretary for the Newcastle

MP Harry Barnes, author of a famous reformist tome, *The Slum: Its Story and Solutions*. During this period he also became embroiled in modernist bohemia, and went to work for Ford Madox Ford's *transatlantic review* in Paris, where he also made the acquaintance of Ezra Pound, the centrifugal driving force and chief organiser of Anglophone literary modernism. Bunting's long friendship with Pound would turn out to be the most meaningful of his artistic career. Pound published Bunting in his Active Anthology of 1931, and integrated him with the American Objectivist school of verse, the first major outbreak of modernist poetry since the early 1920s, which included poets like William Carlos Williams and Louis Zukofsky. Bunting went to live with Pound and W.B. Yeats in Rapallo in Northern Italy in the mid-1930s, and enjoyed a brief period of productivity and literary community before Pound's drift to the extreme right and the increasingly turbulent international climate put an abrupt halt to Bunting's poetic career, at the same time as nearly all of the main currents of thirties modernism were dwindling into irrelevancy.

For Bunting, the Second World War was a much less traumatic experience than its predecessor. Quaker scruples vanished in the face of the fascist threat, and Bunting put in a distinguished stint with the RAF in the Middle East. The immediate post-war period, though, was a time of deep depression and non-productivity. Living with his mother and a young Kurdish wife back in Northumberland, Bunting couldn't find a publisher. The self-proclaimed "Anglican royalist classicist" T.S. Eliot at Faber famously rejected his work on the grounds that it was "too Poundian." Bunting was forced to work long hours on the finance section of the Newcastle *Journal* and *Evening Chronicle* newspapers.

Then, after several years of relative poverty and creative dearth, a dramatic revival occurred in the mid-'60s. While Bunting was being totally ignored by literary London, his connections to the American avant-garde still held good. Pound had helped to arrange the publication of a small collection, *Poems 1950*; in 1964 the Black Mountain writer Jonathan Williams corresponded with a young Geordie beat poet called Tom Pickard, and told him that England's greatest modernist poet was living in obscurity a few miles along the Tyne in a small village called Wylam. Pickard went to visit Bunting immediately and persuaded him to become the centrepiece of poetry readings at the Morden Tower, a dilapidated room in a section of the Newcastle city walls that was transformed into a focal point for the so-called British Poetry Revival. Bunting had, like many of the literary high modernists, always championed a sonically oriented, "musical verse," so this discovery of a flourishing climate of performative poetics proved to be a vital, galvanizing development. Finally given a physical space and a sympathetic audience, Bunting experienced an extraordinary late flowering. In 1964-5 he was finally able compose his masterpiece, a high modernist celebration of Northumbrian culture called *Briggflatts*. This was followed by lecture readings throughout the UK and North America, fellowships at the universities of Newcastle and Durham, and the Northern Arts presidency.

Bunting's struggle to find an audience and a cultural mandate is a case study that shows just how marginalised both modernism and northern culture have been from the mainstream of English letters. With this is mind, it is perhaps no surprise that, given a chance to speak in the progressive, demotic context of sixties Britain, Bunting continually reiterated defenses of Northumbrian identity and autonomy. He talked – only half jokingly – about the desirability of opening up passport control borders at the Humber; he said that the official view of Wordsworth as a magniloquent Romantic-conservative was in part down to the mispronunciation of his verse by "southrons"; he constantly talked about the importance of creating a Northumbrian art conceived in the spirit of ancient models like the Lindisfarne Gospels and Durham Cathedral.

Even Bunting's famous espousals of the need for poetry to be read aloud – in part an inheritance of Pound's belief that verse and music worked best when cultural conditions allowed the two art forms to be "closely knit together" – were often couched in terms that amounted to a rejection of what he perceived to be the bookish, text-oriented culture of the English governing classes:

> All the arts are plagued by charlatans seeking money, or fame, or just an excuse to idle. The less the public understands the art, the easier it is for charlatans to flourish. Since poetry readings became popular, they have found a new field, and it is not easy for the outsider to distinguish the fraud from the poet. But it is a little less difficult when the poem is read aloud. Claptrap soon bores. Threadbare work soon sounds thin and broken backed.
>
> There were mountebanks at the famous Albert Hall meeting [a seminal 1965 poetry "happening" in London], as well as a poet or two, but the worst, most insidious charlatans fill chairs and fellowships at universities, write for the weeklies or work for the BBC or the British Council or some other asylum for obsequious idlers. In the Eighteenth Century it was the Church. If these men had to read aloud in public, their empty lines, without resonance, would soon give them away.

For Bunting, fulfilling Pound's axiomatic insistence on the need to "make it new" was a question of breaking the dominance of the established centres of English officialdom. In sixties Newcastle, this seemed briefly possible. However, his spirit of independence, one that combined genuine localism with modernist internationalism, would once again become a fringe tendency as the social-democracy of post-war era was replaced in the Thatcher era with a renewed emphasis on traditionalism, parochial Englishness, and private wealth preservation.

Bunting published little poetry after *Briggflatts* until his death in Hexham, Northumberland in 1985. But his last project involved research at the Newcastle Literary and Philosophical Institute into the Rising of the North of 1569, an insurrection against Elizabeth I that ended with the execution of 700 Northumbrians and a scorched earth campaign, a reprisal that ensured that much of the far north would be a barren waste land for the next two centuries. An elegy for Bunting written by Tom Pickard describing the circumstances of his death offers a clue to why this particular historical subject might have seemed apposite to Bunting at this juncture:

A flithy winter to have lived through.
Dragged by the hair kicked and kicking into spring.

A year-long miners' strike,
broken.

Police road blocks blocked the motorways
and all roads leading to the north.

*More reactionary than the thirties*
the old fascist-fighting conchie told me[23].

As for Dan Smith, against the backdrop of the 1980s it must have seemed to Bunting as though northern risings – which always seem to offer brief glimpses of how an alternate England might look like – are eternally doomed to be subdued by the authorities whose power base is in London and the south-east.

## When the Whistle Blows

*The Duke can get his rent*
*and we can get our ticket*

*twa pund emigrant*
*on a C.P.R. packet.*
- Basil Bunting, "Gin the Goodwife Stint" (1930).

We are still living in the wake of the failures of Dan Smith and Basil Bunting. For all that New Labour's so-called urban renaissance resulted in a genuine revival of morale across the region – a truly worthwhile achievement – the north-east remains an embattled, peripheral place. It is still a remote outpost in the eyes of the new bastions of English officialdom, as the behaviour of the London media during the Raoul Moat manhunt proved beyond doubt. If any further evidence were needed, in late 2010 it became clear that local councils like Sunderland and South Tyneside would have to make spending cuts ten time those needed to be made by Home Counties localities like Surrey and South Berkshire. The logic of Cameronite neoliberalism, it seemed, favoured the wholesale abandonment of places and people unable to help themselves in these parlous times (and, maybe more importantly, unwilling to provide electoral support for the Tory Party). In a scarcely believable echo of Norman Tebbit's "get on your bike" exhortation of the Thatcher era, in December 2010 the Conservative leader of Buckinghamshire County Council David Shakespeare suggested that one solution to the north's economic worries would be to send some of its unemployed down to the south-east to work as cherry pickers. For Shakespeare, apparently, northerners may be uncouth and idle, but they are, on balance, at least preferable to Romanian immigrants.

Even before Cameron and his New Tories came to power, the postmodern reprisal of post-war regionalism that had been one of the hallmarks of Blairite spin had long been dwindling into farce. John Prescott's well-meaning project for a north-east regional assembly was rejected in a referendum of 2004. Undoubtedly, this indicates that organised regionalism is a contentious issue for much of the local populace. Pro-north sentiment is some way from being translated into popular support for concrete devolutionary proposals. However, the regional assembly project was hardly a cause to galvanise and inspire people into praxis in an era of endemic apathy and widespread disillusionment with the democratic process. An awkward amalgam of corporate interests and New Labour soullessness, the assembly was an ill-thought-out, nebulous idea, hardly worthy of being treated with the democratic gravitas of an official ballot. Many of those who voted at all voted against a Blairism that was increasingly being revealed to be a superficial travesty of the notion of social democracy.

As a revitalised Toryism increasingly occupied centre stage as the '00s unravelled, the demotic mood that had initiated Blairism in the nineties – shallow and patronising though it may have been – became increasingly passé and marginalised. The afore-mentioned rise in popularity of the "boorish northerner" stereotype, particularly in the increasingly mean-spirited world of Brit comedy, was one of the first signs that Cool Britannia's valorisation of football, lad culture, northern slang, and other clichéd working class touchstones was morphing into something more blatantly anti-democratic and patrician. By the time of Cameron's May 2010 election victory, London and the Home Counties ruled supreme over the cultural life of the nation, and visible examples of prosperity in Britain's regions were few and far between (notwithstanding notable exceptions like the newly corporatised bits of Manchester and the *Guardian* travel section's continued patronage of Peak District gastropubs).

Beyond this narrative of neglect, places like the north-east (and, it should go without saying, the north-west, south-west, Scotland, Wales, and Northern Ireland) are harbouring a frustration that right now is only being expressed via the extreme violence of Raoul Moat, or the post-*Braveheart* Hollywood anti-establishment clichés of Ridley Scott. The hope is that the latent spirit of anti-conservative, anti-authoritarian opposition to the monoliths of English tradition that has presided throughout the history of regions like the north-east has not been totally destroyed by the deracinating forces of global capital and thirty years of endemic anti-collectivism. If hoping in this way risks nostalgia, it is at least a form of traditionalism that is quite different from the modern liberal/Tory consensus behind surface "progressivism" and profoundly traditional wealth preservation on the quiet. If England is ever going to change, it is places like the north-east that will have to lead the way in breaking a power structure that ensures the Duke and Duchess of Northumberland are as wealthy and as secure in their fairytale castles as ever before.

# 4

# The Case of Football

*The silly buckets on the deck,*
*That had so long remained,*
*I dreamt that they were filled with dew;*
*And when I awoke, it rained.*
                    - Coleridge, *The Rime of the Ancient Mariner.*

## The Ballad of Newcastle United

It stands to reason that eventually a tipping point will be reached. As the sheer unambiguous *unfairness* of modern Britain becomes more and more apparent to even the most apolitical of folk, something will have to give. Again, it is to culture that we must turn for clues about how and where this spark might come from. We have already seen how folk in the north-east have been forgotten or ignored by the mainstream of English culture. But what of its popular culture today? The popular culture of the north-east is dominated by football. Hence football is a good place to start if we are looking for signs of how the future of the region and its people might pan out.

In north-east football, an oppositional response to exploitation has been a long time coming. The recent history of the region's biggest club, Newcastle United, highlights many of the obstacles to the growth of a bottom-up progressive movement, as well as showing signs of how it might develop in the first place. It deserves outlining at length because it is a parable that resonates throughout contemporary British society and culture as a whole.

For years after the 1997 departure of manager Kevin Keegan – a calamity that ended a short-lived golden age of thrilling if unrewarded attacking football – Newcastle supporters mostly stood by and watched while their club was manhandled by a succession of spectacularly corrupt administrations. Keegan had enjoyed a productive working relationship with his first chairman, Sir John Hall[24]. But when control of NUFC passed to Hall's son Douglas and business-partner Freddy Shepherd around 1996, the magic synthesis of Keeganite idealism and Hallite financial ambition came to an ignominious end. Keegan resigned in the first weeks of 1997, partly in protest at Hall-Shepherd's decision to float the club on the stock market. Not for the last time, an arcane piece of business planning had impacted disastrously on the club.

Managers were appointed, seemingly at random, or because of a slight celebrity reputation, and sacked with an equal lack of explanation. For nearly five years between 1999 and 2004 the club acquired a semblance of stability, with the appointment of local hero and universally lauded former England manager Bobby Robson. Yet inexplicably, after having guided the team to three consecutive top-five league finishes, Robson was removed to make way for Graeme Souness, a notably unpopular and unsuccessful figure. That the aging Robson's final footballing job should have been ended so abruptly and callously was as shocking as it was pointless. But the club's owners had long ago abandoned all ties of sympathy with the supporters and the region. In 1998, Shepherd and Hall were embroiled in a *News of the World* exposé, in which they were recorded in a Spanish brothel referring to Geordie women as "dogs" and calling supporters "mugs" for buying replica shirts in their thousands. After a brief national media furore, a token leave of absence for Shepherd and Hall ended with their return to the board ten months later.

Throughout these events the fans did virtually nothing, perhaps because they had experienced the failure of organised resistance in other contexts only a few years prior to this. The miners' strike and the breaking of the unions in the 1980s were still strong in people's memories. The final death of collective action had been pronounced in the Thatcher years, so the official histories maintained, hence anything that smacked of ideology and political lobbying was likely to be treated with deep suspicion by the average north-east citizen.

On top of this, the region had been offered a vision of how acquiescence with big business might be made to work. The Keegan-John Hall glory days of the early nineties had offered displays of magic to a grey, depressed region just beginning to emerge from one of the worst periods in its history. The closure of the pits and the shipyards had left a sizeable hole in the area's psychological landscape, but football, perhaps the last remaining shibboleth of working class identity, was flourishing in remarkable style. In the wake of Italia '90 and the foundation of the Premier League in 1992, the game was experiencing a moment of new-found confidence and mainstream acceptability, just beginning to come into the sun after years of being a violence-ridden pariah sport. Keegan's and John Hall's exciting, ambitious Newcastle team seemed to encapsulate the mood of optimism in the game at this time, one that paralleled a wider spirit of cultural rejuvenation gathering pace in nineties Britain. To many people in the north- east, and throughout the country, the Keegan-John Hall dream ticket of idealistic, beautiful football combined with an ambitious programme for commercial expansion – superstar signings, major stadium improvements, basketball and ice hockey offshoot teams – seemed to provide a hopeful justification for a neoliberal economic order undergoing the subtle transition from Thatcherism to Blairism. Perhaps private interests really could revitalise a community. The exuberant growth of Newcastle United on and off the pitch in the early to mid-1990s seemed to prove so.

With this in mind, perhaps it is no surprise that even when things began to go awry, as they did following Keegan's departure in 1997, Newcastle supporters remained committed to the idea that the club's power elite should be tolerated for the greater good. When this belief became impossible to maintain, in the wake of the Hall-Shepherd *News of the World* debacle, for example, any sort of substantial organised protest was ruled out on the grounds that it might impact negatively on the team's performance on the pitch. Fans cast their minds back to the 1980s, when the superstar Geordie trio of Peter Beardsley, Chris Waddle, and Paul Gascoigne had been sold by an impoverished club destined for relegation, and they concluded that, however bad things were now, at least there was money in the bank and an impressive new stadium filled to capacity every week. Local hero Alan Shearer had been brought back to the club by Keegan, in a deal brokered by Freddy Shepherd, and his continued presence at the club served to mollify supporter outrage at successive instances of gross mismanagement. Shearer would not be auctioned off to a one of the wealthy Big Clubs, because NUFC was now one of those clubs. Investment was, in a weary cliché of apathetic fanspeak, "for the good of the team." Anyway, the small-scale protests that did take place never seemed to amount to anything.

The sacking of Bobby Robson should have occasioned widespread protest, but by this point inaction and resigned acceptance of the status quo had become endemic. A new crop of nasty, thuggish players added to the mood of disillusionment when they got themselves involved in a series of sex and assault scandals in the mid-'00s. Graeme Souness was sacked in 2006, Glenn Roeder in 2007, Sam Allardyce in 2008. Then the club was subject to a takeover bid, and control passed from Shepherd – by now an utterly vilified figure – to Mike Ashley, owner of the Sports Direct retail empire.

Initial optimism at the Ashley takeover was bolstered when the unpopular Allardyce was sacked and replaced with Keegan himself. At this point, what had been merely a narrative of incompetence and exploitation acquired an air of poetic fantasy. The return of Keegan – who was often, wholly without irony, referred to in the north-east as "The Messiah" – seemed like a confirmation that money could achieve anything. Given free reign, Ashley the mysterious London billionaire, who gave no public speeches and flew into the area on a helicopter on match days, had somehow managed to tap into the region's psyche to pull-off a populist miracle. As in the days of John Hall, community, team, and ownership appeared to be working in harmonious accord, and corporate acquiescence was triumphantly reaffirmed as the only realistic way to run a club. At a press conference to announce his appointment, with delirious fans gathering outside to welcome him, Keegan showed his remarkable understanding of the club's core identity:

> I know the club. I'm not saying the other managers didn't, but I know it as a player, a manager, I know what it's like in terms of what the fans want. They'd like to win something. When they've worked all week, the match for them is like it is for people down south going to the theatre. They want to see something special. They want us to have a go and that's why we're here. We're going to have a go.

With the financial backing of Ashley the magisterial business genius, it looked as though this sort of populist idealism might actually be put into practice.

Soon though, the magic realism that had accompanied Keegan's return to the club was exchanged for absurdist irony. After only eight months as manager, Keegan left the club, later claiming constructive dismissal. Ashley and his Executive Director of Football, the notoriously shady former Chelsea player Dennis Wise, were exposed as cartoon villains who had signed players without Keegan's knowledge and "repeatedly and intentionally misled the press, public, and fans of Newcastle

United," as a later official tribunal concluded. At the same tribunal, an obliviously unrepentant board tried to excuse these actions as "nothing more than an exercise in public relations". Some sort of threshold had been breached. Following Keegan's departure, the team completely collapsed on the pitch. Joe Kinnear, another risible cockney figure, was appointed manager before a heart attack forced him to step down. Then, in a further surreal twist, Alan Shearer took charge for the last ten games of the season, but even he was unable to stop the team being relegated from the Premier League in inglorious fashion. Everything that was sacred to the supporters had been sullied to a scarcely plausible extent. When Ashley announced that the club ground St James's Park was being officially renamed sports-direct.com@St James' Park Stadium, the narrative reached a peak of quasi-fictive ridiculousness that even the most fanciful postmodern novelists could never have dreamed of.

## Movement in the Far Corner: the NUST

What is interesting about the Newcastle United story is its anarchic inability to stop. The actions of both the Shepherd and Ashley administrations seem to suggest that, far from being a cunning elite intent on careful self-preservation, the corporate tendency in charge of modern football is in fact a senseless, guileless force that will ultimately implode because of its own reckless inability to self-limit. The emphasis on Blairite neoliberal compromise that has defined football since the nineties, and that has succeeded in stifling resistance to commercialisation by posing as the only realistic alternative to a world of hooliganism and dilapidated terraces, is being steadily undermined by the vast stupidity of the modern game's powerbrokers. A halfway compromise between business and community interests looks increasingly untenable with each new example of astonishing corruption.

In fact, in subtle ways, in football the tipping point has

arguably already been reached. Conservatism and stigmatisation of collective action are still deep-seated amongst modern football supporters, so much so that only serious provocation would be met with an organised response. But in the case of Newcastle United at least, this provocation was eventually forthcoming. For ordinary, apolitical, apathetic Newcastle supporters, the departure of Kevin Keegan for a second time in September 2008 because of the behaviour of two openly villainous Londoners proved to be the final straw. After this latest debacle, the editors of NUFC fanzines *The Mag* and *True Faith* met and decided to form the Newcastle United Supporters Club, which would soon evolve into the Newcastle United Supporters Trust (NUST), an organisation founded to represent supporter interests.

The trust was created using a model that first appeared in the early 1990s, but which was given national institutional grounding with the foundation of the Supporters' Direct body in 1999/2000, a group that emerged from the third report of the Football Taskforce set up by the Labour government after it came to power in 1997. Of the many moderate achievements of New Labour in office, its involvement in the Football Taskforce and Supporters' Direct initiatives is surely one of the most significant. This basic attempt to empower traditional Labour voters on cultural territory might stand as one of the most meaningful and lasting legacies of the 1997-2010 government, a solid and profound instance of cultural renaissance to contrast with other, more hubristic initiatives. Supporters' Direct provided a burgeoning supporters' trust movement with concrete state legitimacy. Its central suggestion was that trusts should set themselves up as Industrial and Provident Societies (IPSs: essentially latter day versions of co-operative societies).

The foundation of Supporters' Direct meant that when situations of blatant mismanagement and exploitation arose – as at Manchester United in the early '00s, and at Newcastle and Liverpool in 2008 – supporters had a ready-made model for direct, pragmatic collective action. In an age in which de facto unions were still universally, even popularly loathed, and in which further consolidations of private sector power were still ongoing and seemingly unstoppable, this emergence of a government-sanctioned programme for cooperative-style activity was nothing short of remarkable. Because it is only culture, perhaps this de jure collectivism via the backdoor has been overlooked as a marginal irrelevancy. Also notable is the fact that supporters' trusts tend to play down the ideological connotations of their activities, with most being at pains to point out that they are not political lobby groups. But political they most certainly are. The ambitions of the trusts go beyond the mere representation of community interests: their ultimate goal is fan ownership on the continental model popular in countries like Spain and Germany.

With the English Premier League turning in a total profit of £2 billion every year (by far the most lucrative in the world) the wide-reaching political implications of even a moderate increase in fan ownership emerging from a cooperative-style movement cannot be underestimated. It is difficult to imagine, for example, Rupert Murdoch having anything like the level of influence he currently enjoys in Britain were football clubs to be placed in the hands of supporters, who could hardly condone the sort of consumer exploitation Murdoch's BSkyB has exercised over fans since the Premier League's foundation in 1992. This sort of popular confrontation of private interests would be a genuinely remarkable development in recent British political history. Since the Thatcher era, it has at times been impossible to see an end to the destruction of civic enfranchisement through the expansion of private interests. But increasingly, an alternative to powerlessness and to the view that cultural institutions must be run along competitive, market-driven models seems not only possible, but inevitable. When an otherwise moderate folk populace begins to form collectivist organisations spontaneously and unselfconsciously, and when that activity is aided and abetted by the British Labour party, it seems clear that a subtle and profound change has taken place.

## Sparks Fly Upward

Where should we look for the first signs of a thaw in the neoliberal winter? At the intellectual end of the spectrum, the situation is parlous, but not hopeless. New plutocratic command of the media and cultural mainstream is still formidable. However, the decline of print media is creating ever more copious openings for an internet-based intelligentsia to flourish, and a climate of subversion and critique is burgeoning as a result. The recent demonstrations in London against the rise in tuition fees proved that there is great scope for an alliance of students and intellectuals utilising the potential of online blogs and social networking tools. With Cameron in power, middle-class liberal Britain is becoming more and more squeamish about neoliberalism, its Siamese twin throughout the Blair-Brown years. Perhaps a newly efficacious counter-culture will emerge from these establishment fringes: from a web-based avant-garde, from an academia fighting for its autonomy.

Yet for truly social-democratic change to occur, this tendency will have to rekindle unity with some form of bottom-up movement. Political parties all over the West have alternately suffered from and made political capital out of a perceived rise in "metropolitan elitism" in recent years. To challenge the deep inequalities of the neoliberal economy, we need to look further than the radical margins of bourgeois metropole, while at the same time not falling into the trap of anti-cosmopolitan chauvinism. The British left-intelligentsia has, for the most part, been cut off from a populist grassroots; one of the most tragic ruptures to have taken place over the last 30 years has been this severing of the proletariat from an educated, unionised lower-middle-class. As a result, one of the greatest pitfalls to avoid will be the replication of an elitist power dynamic through a top-down imposition of ideology, and conversely, trying not to succumb to an over eager anti-elitism that proffers separatism at the cost of a truly common culture. Emphasis on the potential of an intellectual avant-garde to make reforming inroads is not enough, and neither is the blind affirmation of single-class interests. For a really effective opposition to emerge, an alliance between the working class and the intelligentsia must somehow be reinstated. Without two-way movement between these two groups, populist terrain will very quickly become the preserve of the far right. A UK version of the US Tea Party is not so difficult to imagine, as the recent emergence of the English Defence League shows.

One major difference though between Britain and the US, one crucial obstacle standing in the way of a Tea Party-style right-populism, is the fact that, insofar as popular collectivism still exists in this country, it exists as a memory of an earlier epoch in which social democracy was genuine and comprehensive. It is hardly backward-looking to suggest that the renewed willingness to organise and to resist that is evident in the case of football is the expression of a not-quite-obsolescent egalitarian heritage in the first tentative stages of revival.

Inherited contemporary commonplaces are a big part of the problem. For instance, far too often the bourgeois fear of crowds has coloured the view of both football and working class culture as a whole, even amongst otherwise intelligent voices. The facile association of crowds and far right politics popularised by theorists like Theodor Adorno in the post-World War II period is still the dominant tendency in leftist discourse, a further instance of disconnect between even the most sympathetic intelligentsia commentators and a newly anathematised working class[25]. Hence, the usually sensible critic Terry Eagleton could rehearse the old "opium of the people" argument in a *Guardian* article of 2010:

Modern societies deny men and women the experience of solidarity, which football provides to the point of collective delirium ... Nobody serious about political change can shirk the fact that the game has to be abolished.

Similarly, J.G. Ballard, in one of his last published articles ("A Fascist's Guide to Premiership", *New Statesman*, 2006), could look at the preponderance of St George flags on a drive from Shepperton to Heathrow and conclude that

[t]his wasn't patriotism so much as a waking sense of tribal identity, dormant for decades. The notion of being British has never been so devalued. Sport alone seems able to be the catalyst of significant social change. Football crowds rocking stadiums and bellowing anthems are taking part in political rallies without realising it, as would-be fascist leaders will have noted.

The English, thank God, have always detested jackboots, searchlight parades and Führers ranting from balconies. But the Premier League, at the pinnacle of our entertainment culture, is a huge engine of potential change, waiting to be switched on. Could consumerism evolve into fascism? There is nothing to stop some strange consumer trend becoming a new ideology.

There is no doubting that fascism and football have often overlapped, or that football is, in many cases, a soporific leisure pastime that travesties the notion of solidarity. But such arguments are deeply lopsided. Is football, as Ballard argues, merely a "strange consumer trend"? Is Eagleton right to see football as a "distraction from political injustice" one in which "[b]lind loyalty and an internecine rivalry gratify some of our most powerful evolutionary instincts"?

When reading accounts like these, I'm reminded of hearing

Germaine Greer try to jazz up Shakespeare at a sixth-form English conference by saying that a scene in *Hamlet* was "a bit like when Beckham kicks a corner for Manchester." Like Greer, on some basic level, both Ballard and Eagleton have spectacularly misjudged the nature and vocabulary of the game. Their assertions are those of outsiders unable to view a complex art form and social phenomenon with subtlety, like the classical music buff who thinks pop music is just so much racket and noise. That two broadly leftist writers should end up retreading an old-fashioned mystification like this is ironic and unfortunate. In such critiques, large groups of people are reimagined as undifferentiated masses, moronic crowds susceptible to the manipulations of a superior capitalist elite (or else the sweeping, suave phraseology of a Ballard or an Eagleton). The folk are returned to the status of a singular *Volk*, a lumpen body liable to resort to fascism and neo-primitivism at the first available opportunity.

Actually, reading these arguments against the grain yields some interesting results. Eagleton comments that the "vivid sense of tradition [in football] contrasts with the historical amnesia of postmodern culture." And if we are able to see beyond the automatic assumption that this is another opiate-style desublimation, we might suggest that football's anti-postmodern historical sense is something valuable, something that might be nudged into positivity and used as a foundation for a revival of a collective culture. Similarly, Eagleton contrasts football with the old European tradition of popular carnival, which "could be a genuinely anarchic affair, a foretaste of a classless society." Might not football be making a similar evocation? The sorts of tribalism and solidarity evident in the contemporary game may often be of a negative kind. But as the supporters' trusts movement shows, there are also plenty of instances of supporter solidarity translating into bona fide grassroots activism. If we are hoping to revive solidarity on a popular scale, shouldn't we look to instances where it is still extant, however faintly, rather than hoping to magic it out of thin air? Such attempts may invite accusations of nostalgia, but the alternative is the total repudiation of heritage and folk-memory. This denial of a collective history is an identity-annulling strategy that has served neoliberalism and postmodern culture exceedingly well.

## The Assumption of Ugliness

Ballard's prophecy of consumerism morphing into fascism with football as the handmaiden of change is a compelling one ("a huge engine of potential change, waiting to be switched on"). As the fallout from the Raoul Moat manhunt showed, a gathering feeling of populist anger at the scarcely-articulated injustices of neoliberalism might easily tip over into something very ugly indeed. But this automatic *assumption* of ugliness is what must be avoided at all costs. It seems clear that the default tendency to see the modern-day proletariat as a vulgar fringe on the brink of violent revolt is one of the consequences of a society that has become almost irretrievably divided without even knowing it. To borrow the terminology of late-twentieth century critical theory, we have lost all tolerance for the Other, all compunction to sympathise and to deconstruct media myths. The maniacal pursuit of personal happiness that is the hallmark of the consumerist dream is so univocal and dominant that the inevitable flipside – the harsh negativity directed at the Vicky Pollards and the moronic football supporters of little Britain – has gradually developed into a counter-balancing hysteria. Denied an outlet for directing our anger at the real architects of exploitation, we turn inwards, cynically dismantling anything that does not conform to the realities of the capitalist status quo, destroying with an urbane, satirical flourish the "us" that might be our liberation.

What if we assumed the opposite? What if we interpreted Ballard's view of football as an engine of potential change in the way you might think people would: as an affirmative statement of possibility? What if we started from the premise that football supporters are profoundly committed to solidarity, just waiting for the glimmer of a chance to put this commitment into action? The recent activity of football organizations at Newcastle, Liverpool, Manchester United, and Arsenal provides tangible support for this theory; democratic collective resistance, and not fascistic extremism, seems to be the most common working-class response to the corruptions of a capitalist elite that looks increasingly, anarchically unhinged. There are very few cultural outlets for the disparate, disenfranchised new proletariat of the early-twenty-first century. The anti-democratic, anti-egalitarian currents of the last thirty years have ensured this, turning popular and folk culture into travestied inversions of their former selves. But when we do see people organizing themselves, the signs are, or should be, incredibly positive. We should think seriously about why conversations about football and football fans are always coloured by scepticism, condescension, and ridicule. What is this pessimism holding in check? Whose interests are being served by it?

The fate of the opposition to a political mainstream that is now plainly, unambiguously Thatcherite and anti-populist will depend on its ability to treat the British folk as a complex, variegated entity, but one that is nevertheless a definite common reality capable of self-actuating change. The example of the revival of community activism discernible in football culture needs gate-keeping representatives if it is to burgeon into something genuinely effective and widespread. There are very modest harbingers that certain sectors of the Labour Party understand that the future of the left lies in renewing old alliances between communities and mainstream politics, not in the patently spurious manner of Cameron's Big Society or the frankly ridiculous "Blue Labour" theory advocated by Lord Maurice Glasman, but by providing basic, pragmatic support and representation for causes like the supporters' trust movement.

One such example is Chi Onwurah, Labour MP for Newcastle Central. Onwurah came to office in the 2010 election, and hence is not tainted by association with the Blair/Brown years. A former electrical engineer, as shadow minister for business, innovation, and skills Onwurah has been an articulate critic of government funding cuts for the UK Resource Centre for Women in Science Engineering and Technology. She is also a Newcastle United Supporters Trust board member. In links like this, in figures that revivify and reorient core Labour principles in a patient, constructive way, we should invest a great deal of hope.

There are, of course, forceful reasons to doubt mainstream political avenues. Another, much more ambivalent figure in the vanguard of Labour Party ideological renewal is Andy Burnham. In many respects Burnham is the archetypal odious Blairite. After becoming an MP in 2001, Burnham was a staunch backer of the Iraq war and identity cards. In the grey twilight years of New Labour, as Secretary of State for Culture, Media, and Sport (2008-9) he made lickspittle overtures to the music industry lobby group UK Music. As Health Secretary (2009-10) he threw himself wholeheartedly into the foundation hospitals fiasco. This record is not suggestive of a man able to think outside the box of New Labour orthodoxy.

Yet for all his unfortunate recent history, in the Labour leadership election debates of 2010, Burnham stood out because of an ability to offer plausible, practical suggestions for Labour re-engagement with its onetime grassroots base. Burnham's implorations for a "New Mutualism" at first sight seemed like a mere continuation of Blairite spin. But in fact the phrase has an interesting etymology. In the late 1990s, before becoming an MP, Burnham worked as an adviser for the Football Taskforce, and was a key figure in the creation of Supporters' Direct in 1999, which he chaired from 2002-5. Part of the theoretical backdrop to the foundation of SD, along with the taskforce report, was a Co-operative Party pamphlet called "New Mutualism: A Golden

Goal? Uniting Supporters and their Clubs" by the economist Jonathan Michie, who would later become a pivotal figure in Shareholders' United (an organisation that blocked Rupert Murdoch's takeover of Man United in 1998 and would later morph into the club's supporters' trust).

Burnham's revival of the New Mutualist slogan over a decade later is therefore a notable instance of New Labour's effective stance on football being used latterly as the basis for a more wide-reaching political praxis. Sweep away the Blairite residue, and there is a flicker of promise about the still relatively young Andy Burnham. In the 2010 leadership debates, his talk of an "aspirational socialism" might have had a faint Thatcherite ring to it, but on the other hand it managed to sneak the word socialism into discussions that were otherwise astonishingly timid, Fabian-esque, and even occasionally – because of David Miliband's lingering presence – consummately right-wing. Building on the supporters' trust movement, attacking the "London context" of a nepotistic work-experience culture and the "postcode lottery," defending comprehensive schools with partisan earnestness: Burnham's understanding of the basic egalitarian-populist potential in areas like this offers a very elementary model for how Labour might go about recovering its ideological soul.

**Why We're Here**
Again it bears repeating that the situation is poised on a knife-edge. Even if folk sentiment does not find an outlet in neo-fascism or serial-killing outlaws, it can easily be used in the service of more moderately conservative causes. As evinced by the failure of the north-east assembly referendum in 2004, and the rejection of proposals for public transport improvements in Manchester in 2009, popular support for civic causes is regularly undermined by popular indifference, selfishness and cynicism, even in places where communitarian culture remains relatively

strong. Moreover, as these examples show, the Labour Party is fundamentally hampered by the fact that it has itself been a staunchly anti-egalitarian, anti-populist force in British society in recent times, for all its meticulously honed surface-image of tubthumping folksiness. Perhaps the deep-seated gaps in demography, which opened up in the Thatcher era and were compounded by New Labour's commitment to nurturing a new liberal elite cannot be bridged. Perhaps Ed Miliband is too blandly technocratic, urbane, and mandarin to have even the faintest inkling about a folk-populace, the sort of man far more likely to be seen at a Mumford and Sons gig than a football match.

But, with or without the Labour Party, at this moment of change and renewal it is imperative that we begin the long uphill struggle back to a position where we see the essence of socialism in the profound metaphor that inheres in the word *folk*. Deconstructive cynicism has had its day. Timidity in invoking communitarian sentiment has got us nowhere. We believe unequivocally in our existence as individuals, and that this is something worth fighting for. Why shouldn't we invest a similar level of belief in our existence as part of a team? We have to recognise that a common heritage and future defined by the comprehensive empowerment of a broadly defined folk is something that has to be boldly and unapologetically asserted, even if this notion can and should always be subject to qualification, caveats, and the nuances of intelligent discourse. Without this belief, in a very real sense, we will cease to exist. Remarks made by Raymond Williams in a book published in 1956 are even more pertinent to our situation today:

> The inequalities of many kinds which still dominate our community make effective communication difficult or impossible. We lack a genuinely common experience, save in certain rare and dangerous moments of crisis. What we are paying

for this lack, in every kind of currency, is now sufficiently evident. We need a common culture, not for the sake of an abstraction, but because we shall not survive without it[26].

The reclamation of folk sentiment and folk opposition from the right-wing margins and from the ironic, belittling forces of bourgeois consumerism is every bit as serious as this. Re-emphasising the legitimacy of a common culture founded in ordinary, elemental solidarity will not be an easy task. But we have to at least try. In the words of Kevin Keegan, the former manager of Newcastle United: "They want us to have a go, and that's why we're here. We're going to have a go."

# Notes

1.  This was later disputed by numerous NUFC supporters in attendance at the game.
2.  See http://thequietus.com/articles/04642-raoul-moat-the-ugly-truth-about-folk-heroism-and-spotify-playlist
3.  It is at least in part a soundbite reduction of the "Red Toryism" advocated by political thinker Philip Blond. Arguably, Cameron's ultra-vague "Big Society" has finally exposed the oxymoronic nature of Blond's theory.
4.  See George Orwell, "England Your England" (1941).
5.  See Thompson, *The Makings of the British Working Class* (1963), Hobsbawm, "The Making of the Working Class 1870-1914" (1984), and Hoggart, *The Uses of Literacy* (1957).
6.  The continued stigma attached to unionization in contemporary Britain is baffling, bearing in mind that unions have wielded almost zero influence in British society throughout the working lives of the vast majority of the present-day workforce. The right-wing ability to conjure the ghost of an aggressive Trade Union movement is a frankly miraculous achievement.
7.  See also Ricky Gervais's enthusiastic adoption of "boorish northerner" stereotype Karl Pilkington as part of his podcast comedy act.
8.  In fact, Lloyd Weber actually went the whole hog on the TV talent show *Over the Rainbow*, munificently appraising nubile young female singers from a golden throne.
9.  Poshness in pop music is a convoluted issue, blighted by hypocrisy. There was something undeniably perverse about the old middle-class music press's habit of ridiculing musicians from affluent backgrounds, its fetish for the "authenticity" of working-class art. Yet there was also something valid and necessary in this leveling impulse.

Today's depoliticised, anti-literate music press seems to have no real qualms about elitism, perhaps because the music press itself is now not only middle-class but exclusively, nepotistically so: a finishing school for those members of the new plutocracy dedicated to the modern ideal of a hedonistic lifestyle married to an aggressive, hyper-ambitious career. With this is mind, it is predictable that the univocal elitism of the Mumford and Friends network should pass by largely without comment.

10. The foundation of an Oxfordshire cheese-making business by Alex James – the loathsome former Blur bassist – was another similar instance of post-industrial fairytale-migration.

11. The latter-day retro craze for beards has been astutely examined by bloggers Simon Reynolds and Zone Styx Travelcard (http://blissout.blogspot.com/2009/11/more-on-beards-wouldyabelieve-it.html; http://zonestyxtravelcard.blogspot.com/2009/11/beards-per-minute.html)

12. See Calvin Harris's tacky electro anthem of 2007, "Acceptable in the Eighties," a tune that sums up the auto-erotic proclivities of this generation pretty well.

13. This is not to say that the post-war folk revival does not have a meaningful ongoing legacy. Contemporary artists like The Unthanks and Chris Wood are only the most visible examples of a folk tradition that continues to combine political radicalism and experimentation with an appreciation of the heritage of British popular song in both its rural and urban incarnations. Particularly noteworthy examples include Chris Wood's song "Hollow Point" about the Jean Charles de Menezes killing, and The Unthanks' covers of Robert Wyatt and baroque reinterpretations of north-east industrial ballads.

14. Like the Marlings (see previous chapter), the Percys could trace a lineage back to William the Conqueror.

15. In opposition, the north-east had played a key role in the Blairite PR charm offensive. See Blair's enthusiastic foreword to Paul Joannou's 1995 book *Newcastle United: The First Hundred Years and More*, an amusing example of the Blair campaign's attempts to establish his Geordie credentials. Also notable from a regional point of view is the fact that Blair's iconic 1997 "people's princess" speech was delivered in a "grassroots" context at his Sedgefield constituency in County Durham.

16. The comically awkward moniker NewcastleGateshead is still in use as of 2011, a lasting legacy of the preceding decade's botched corporatism.

17. Parliamentary seats in the north-east between 1997 and 2010 averaged out as follows: 1 Conservative, 1 Lib Dem, 27 Labour.

18. With some notable exceptions, discussions of "Englishness" were typically muddled, if not wholly spurious. Endorsements of Englishness were often based on the pseudo-revisionist premise that the English had been passed over in an era of post-colonialism and political correctness (see, for example, Jeremy Paxman's *The English*, Alexandra Harris's *Romantic Moderns*, and Andrew Motion's risible 2011 poem "Redcrosse" - particularly apposite because of its casual appropriation of the word "folk" to the cause of coffee-table nationalism). According to this view, the traditional English identity had become a marginal, forgotten cause. As the previous chapter argued, with hindsight it seems obvious that this revival of interest in English nationalist myths was the natural precursor to the emergence and final triumph of the New Tories and their cultural mode, Green Toryism.

19. See also Ricky Gervais's *Extras* show-within-show, *When The Whistle Blows*, which featured an imbecilic northern protagonist in a stereotyped kitchen-sink setting, and which was

intended to represent a dumbed-down, populist travesty of lead-character Andy's sophisticated artistic ambitions.

20. As of February 2011, the weekly pay gap between highest and lowest earners was £392. In London it is nearly double that (£686). See http://www.dailyfinance.co.uk/2011/02/21/wealth-gap-narrower-in-north/

21. In this passage I am drawing heavily on information provided in Owen Hatherley's article, "Tyneside Modernism", 3:am Magazine, http://www.3ammagazine.com/3am/tyneside-modernism/.

22. See Peter Quatermain, *Basil Bunting: Poet of the North* (1990).

23. See Tom Pickard, *Hole in the Wall: New and Selected Poems* (2002).

24. Hall is an ambivalent figure. An arch-Thatcherite robber-baron who provided the inspiration for a nefarious character in early drafts of Peter Flannery's 1996 TV drama *Our Friends in the North*, Hall was also a staunch regionalist with a mitigating knack for populism and fan sentiment.

25. See Theodor Adorno, "Freudian Theory and the Pattern of Fascist Propaganda" (1951).

26. See Raymond Williams, *Culture and Society: 1780-1950* (1958).

# Acknowledgements

Iona Niven, Louise Weston, Ol Escritt, Graeme Ferguson, Grant Edgeworth, Tom Astley, Paul McGuire, Ernie, Eileen, Champ, Ellen and John McWilliams, Bob Pringle, Noreen Hughes, Aaron Rosenberg and Daisy Parente, Iason and Fatin, Hugh, Ed, Steve, Dave, Michelle, Alys, Oren, David, Tom Tracey, John L, John F, Angus, Alex, Johannes and Sonja, The Weston Family, The Dunne Family, Janet, Adrian, Harry, Lewis Greener, The Toland Family, The O'Neills, Laura Waugh, Dan English, Mark Howat, Neesham, Al Neal, Wilson, Drew, Jack, Sills, Magdalena Reid, Chloe Reed, Esther, Rosie Thomas, Becky Unthank, David Oliver, Chris Wood, Alistair Anderson, Pete Cooper, Ian Carr, Emma Reid, Peter Tickell, Will Lee, Kevin Hodgson, The Ward Family, John Moore, Len Young, Alison, Sian, Rhoda, Shannon Fitzpatrick, Katie Bamber, Ryan, Laura, Sophie, Kate, Andrew Roberts, Sam Sharpe, Scott, Rhian, Robbie, Kate Killeen, Lisa, Lisa, Phil, Mike, Rob, Gemma, Dave Haslam, Luke Smith, Justin Lockey, Ollie Smith, The Yeldings, The Astley Family, Mariley, Rita Sutherland, Cynthia Orange, Cathy Carter, Tim Kendall, George Donaldson, John Lee, Moira Megaw, Tony Boorman, Alistair and Simon Walker, The Volsens, The Lognonne Family, Andrew Hodgson, Gareth Moore, Tom Pickard, Ron Bush, Charlotta Salmi, Caroline and Ursula Neal, Ian Inglis, Tommy Gradwell, Colin Smith, Philip Leadbitter, Gale Watson, Mark Crinson, David O'Connor, Gillian Spendiff, Sheena Moore, Suzanne Addavide, The Veitch Family, The Smith Family, Fiona McGuire, The Hanley Family, Barney Jones, Paul Loraine, Tariq and Emma Goddard, Owen Hatherley, Carl Neville, Mark Fisher, Tom May.

Contemporary culture has eliminated both the concept of the public and the figure of the intellectual. Former public spaces – both physical and cultural – are now either derelict or colonized by advertising. A cretinous anti-intellectualism presides, cheerled by expensively educated hacks in the pay of multinational corporations who reassure their bored readers that there is no need to rouse themselves from their interpassive stupor. The informal censorship internalized and propagated by the cultural workers of late capitalism generates a banal conformity that the propaganda chiefs of Stalinism could only ever have dreamt of imposing. Zer0 Books knows that another kind of discourse – intellectual without being academic, popular without being populist – is not only possible: it is already flourishing, in the regions beyond the striplit malls of so-called mass media and the neurotically bureaucratic halls of the academy. Zer0 is committed to the idea of publishing as a making public of the intellectual. It is convinced that in the unthinking, blandly consensual culture in which we live, critical and engaged theoretical reflection is more important than ever before.